The Ascott Martyrs

The Ascott Martyrs

Sixteen women from Ascott-under-Wychwood
who were sent over the hills to glory

―――※―――

Beverley McCombs

Writes Hill
2016

First published 2016
Published by Writes Hill Press Limited
PO Box 23 032, Wellington 6140, New Zealand
www.writeshillpress.co.nz

© Beverley McCombs, 2016

ISBN 978-0-9922603-8-5

All rights reserved. Except for any fair dealing for the purposes of private study, research, or review as permitted under the New Zealand Copyright Act 1994, no part of this publication may be reproduced, stored in a retrieval system or transmitted in any form or by any means, electronic, mechanical, photocopying, recorded or otherwise, without the prior written permission of the publisher and copyright holder.

Edited by Anne Else
Cover and book design Writes Hill Press
Printed by printing.com

Back flap image: The author with her sister, Judith, sitting on the current commemorative seat around the horse chestnut tree in Ascott-under-Wychwood. Photo by Robert Salmon.
Cover image: Beverley McCombs (Photo by Forrest Smyth, Virtual Silver)
Village background image: Ascott-under-Wychwood.
Please note: Unless otherwise indicated, the photos are by the author.

CONTENTS

ACKNOWLEDGEMENTS vii
INTRODUCTION: Finding the story 1
CHAPTER 1: VILLAGE LIFE. Ascott-under-Wychwood 8
CHAPTER 2: WORKING LIFE. Gloving, domestic service, farming 17
CHAPTER 3: THE UNION. 'Disrespectful, vexatious and riotous' 25
CHAPTER 4: ON STRIKE. Farm labourers unite 30
CHAPTER 5: IN COURT. The trial of the 'agricultural Amazons' 35
CHAPTER 6: THE RIOT. 'Pull down the police station!' 43
CHAPTER 7: SENTENCED. Prison with hard labour 48
CHAPTER 8: COPING AT HOME. The women's families 52
CHAPTER 9: RELEASED. 'They be martyrs to a good cause' .. 55
CHAPTER 10: LEGAL REFORM. The magistrates criticised 62
CHAPTER 11: SENTENCE UNDER SCRUTINY. Change on the horizon 66
CHAPTER 12: MOTHERING IN PRISON. The treatment of the women and their babies 72
CHAPTER 13: RALLYING. Celebrations and rewards 77
CHAPTER 14: FUTURE IMPACT. The women's legacy 80
EPILOGUE: Keeping the story alive 85

BIOGRAPHIES: The sixteen women who were sent to prison
- Levia (Lavinia) Dring 89
- Fanny Honeybone 92
- Amelia Moss 93
- Ann Moss 95
- Ann Susan Moss 96
- Caroline Moss 97
- Charlotte Moss 98
- Jane Moss 100
- Martha Moss 102
- Mary Moss 105
- Elizabeth Pratley 106
- Ellen Pratley 108
- Mary Pratley 111
- Martha Smith 114
- Mary Moss (otherwise Smith) 116
- Rebecca Smith 118

ENDNOTES 122

BIBLIOGRAPHY 134

INDEX OF NAMES 138

ACKNOWLEDGEMENTS

I would like to thank all those who have helped me throughout the whole project of telling the Ascott martyrs' story: with my research, with the writing, with getting it into shape for publication, and with support and encouragement.

With regard to Britain, in particular I would like to thank the staff at the Oxfordshire Archives, the Museum of Labour History in Manchester, the Centre for Oxfordshire Studies, and members of the Wychwoods Local History Society, Oxfordshire Family History Society, Finstock Local History Society, Vale of the White Horse branch of the Berkshire Family History Society, and Stratford-on-Avon Local History Society. My heartfelt thanks go also to those unseen people who, over many years, have transcribed the parish registers and made them available.

I would also like to thank the numerous groups, in both Britain and New Zealand, who have invited me to talk about the Ascott martyrs at their gatherings.

Many individuals have been helpful and supportive in numerous ways. They include the late Rollo Arnold, Wendy Archer, Hazel Bagworth-Mann, Jon Carpenter, Elizabeth Finn, Andrew Flinn, Diane Hawke, Michelle Hawke, Roger Hepworth, Linda Hilsdon, J. R. Hodgkins, Joan Howard-Drake, Paul and Pauline Jackson, Joan and Hugh Kearsey, Alison Kirkman, Vivian Lochhead, Charlotte Macdonald, Tom McQuay, the late Ralph Mann, John Martin, Susan Matthews, the late Eric Moss, Robert Newton, Wendy and Jim Pearse, Jock Phillips, John Rawlins, F. R. Ryley, the late Robert and Sheila Salmon, Claire Toynbee, Harvey Warner, Margaret Ware, Duncan Waugh and Belinda Willson.

Thanks also to Anne Else, my editor, to whom I will be forever grateful for her endless patience, kindness, and excellent editing skills, as well as ensuring that this book was completed.

Most importantly, my heartfelt thanks and appreciation to my husband, Peter, who has encouraged my involvement in this project from that very first visit to the Oxfordshire Archives in the basement of the Oxford City Council building, on through finding so many people and places involved with this story. My family has heard this story over many years, and I thank them for their patience and their belief that I would get this book finished.

Beverley McCombs
2016

INTRODUCTION

FINDING the STORY

The day was sunny and the sea blue and calm as I stood on the rocky Lizard Peninsula on the southwest coast of England. As I looked towards the horizon, a wave of deep sadness washed over me. Was this an echo of the collective grief of my forebears, as they looked ahead to an unknown future and then turned back for a last view of their homeland? Why did they leave this 'green and pleasant land' and embark on a long voyage to the other side of the world?

One of them was my great-grandmother, 19-year-old Jane Pratley (née Malins). She sailed to New Zealand in 1874 on the clipper ship *Crusader*, with her new husband, Eli Pratley, nearly ten years her senior, and her stepdaughter, three-year-old Ellen. Jane was Eli's second wife, born in Wyre Piddle, near Throckmorton, Worcestershire. They had married in the village of Ascott-under-Wychwood, in the neighbouring county of Oxfordshire, where Eli's family had lived for many years.

In 1988 my husband, Peter, and I went to Ascott-under-Wychwood to see where Eli came from. We did not really expect to find anything related to his family. There were no written records and we would be lucky to find a Pratley headstone in the village churchyard. They were farm labourers, on the lowest rung of England's social ladder. In 1872 Lloyd Jones, a keen supporter of trade unionism, wrote of the agricultural labourer:

> In intellect he is a child, in position a helot, in condition a squalid outcast, he knows nothing of the past; his knowledge of the future is limited to the field he works in ... the Squire is his king, the Parson his deity, the taproom his conception of earthly bliss.[1]

We turned off the A361 between Chipping Norton and Burford into London Lane and approached the village, a quiet little country place on the edge of the Cotswolds. As we drove closer, we noticed that the ploughed fields reminded us of those in South Canterbury, New Zealand, where Eli and Jane eventually settled.

Holy Trinity, the Church of England parish church, was easy to find as it was on higher ground than the rest of the village. We entered the church gate and walked along a pathway lined with tall lime trees. The church door was locked, so we wandered around the churchyard looking for a gravestone with a familiar name, particularly that of Eli's first wife, Elizabeth. But we found nothing. We consoled ourselves by imagining Eli and Jane's wedding in the church.

Still somewhat dispirited, we went into the only shop we could see, in the front room of a house on the corner of High Street and London Lane. The shopkeeper recognised us as strangers and asked what brought us there.

'I've come to see the church where my great-grandparents were married,' I answered. 'What was their name?' she asked. 'Pratley,' I replied. 'Not another one,' she said bluntly. 'Have you seen the tree over there on the village green?'

The horse chestnut tree stood alone in the centre of the green. As we got closer we could see that an eight-sided wooden seat had been built around it. Attached to the seat on one side was a memorial plaque:

> This seat was erected to celebrate the centenary of the 'Ascott Martyrs', the sixteen women of Ascott who were sent to prison in 1873 for the part they played in the founding of the Agricultural Workers Union when they were sent 'over the hills to glory'.

Above the plaque were the names Levia Dring and Celia Honeybone. The other seven seats had two names each: Elizabeth Honeybone and Eliza Honeybone; Fanny Honeybone and Mrs Caleb Moss; Charlotte Moss and Mary Moss; Caroline Moss and Anna Moss; Mrs William Moss and Jane Pratley; Mary Pratley and Nelly Pratley; Becky Smith and Martha Smith.

Three Pratley names. Were they related to me? And all those Mosses—Eli's mother was Jemima Moss, so maybe they were also related to me. I had not heard of any Agricultural Workers' Union—what part had these women played in its founding? I also wondered what 'Ascott martyrs' might mean. Were they true martyrs who paid the penalty of death? I didn't know what 'over the hills to glory' meant either. Surely, sixteen women who went away 'over the hills' must have left many children to be looked after. Just having a memorial to a group of women was uncommon for that period.

INTRODUCTION

The horse chestnut tree on the village green with the original wooden seat and the plaques bearing the names of the 'Ascott martyrs'.

Ascott martyrs... why had I not heard anything about this before? Perhaps here was an answer as to why Eli and Jane had left England for New Zealand in 1874. I could see there was some research to do, with the plaque as my template and guide. I felt the lure of the village and its past beckon me. 'Tell our story,' the women seemed to say.

At that stage I did not know that the Ascott martyrs would dominate my life for years to come. Delving into their story, I came to understand and appreciate that my great-grandfather Eli Pratley and his second wife, Jane, had come to New Zealand to escape the oppression of the English class system, which they had so forcibly experienced. Instead of being faintly ashamed of my 'unimportant' lowly ancestors, I came to respect and admire them.

Eli became a determined immigrant. In 1873, with the encouragement of the new Agricultural Labourers' Union, he took his family to Canada, where his first wife, Elizabeth, died. He returned to Ascott, England, with his children, and the next year, with his new wife, Jane, and his daughter, Ellen, set out again, this time on the 96-day voyage to New Zealand where Eli rose from farm labourer to landowner. He and Jane raised eleven boys and two daughters. One of their sons, William, was my grandfather.

This book tells the remarkable story of sixteen ordinary English village women and their families. In the spring of 1873, they tried to stop two youths from another village working in place of their menfolk, who were on strike. It was this action that would see the women tried, convicted, 'sent over the hills', imprisoned with hard labour, and celebrated as martyrs. I discovered that 'Over the Hills to Glory' was an English country dance with a catchy tune played on the fiddle. It was also the signature tune of a play of the same name by Doris Warner, which tells the story of the Ascott martyrs, much of the dialogue taking place among the women as they sit making gloves to earn a little money. Written in 1953, the play was performed in several villages of the district in the 1980s. Doris explained 'going over the hills' was the wry way the old folk referred to being sent to Chipping Norton, either to prison (as in the case of the sixteen women) or to the workhouse.

INTRODUCTION

It was Doris's husband, Ivor Warner, who in 1973, to celebrate the centenary of the women's actions, funded the planting of the horse chestnut tree on the Ascott-under-Wychwood village green, and the building of the octagonal wooden seat around it, with the names of sixteen women who were then believed to have been involved. This memorial, the one Peter and I saw in 1988, played a major part in keeping the women's story alive.

In June 2000, that wooden seat was replaced with a new four-sided metal one, as a village project to mark the new millennium. Each of the four sides of this seat bears an inscription. One side has the words, 'Ascott Martyrs imprisoned 1873'. It was felt that this new inscription was more accurate than the original plaque. In hindsight, it was a pity that it omitted the reference to the Agricultural Workers' Union, as further research makes it clear that the women did indeed play a part in the early days of the union, giving it much needed national publicity and opportunities for its leaders to expound its principles and virtues. The women's experience encouraged the agricultural labourers to have a voice and take advantage of the benefits of unionising.

The names of the women listed on the charge sheets are inscribed on another two sides of the new seat. One lists Amelia Moss, Caroline Moss, Jane Moss, Martha Moss, Mary Moss, Ellen Pratley, Elizabeth Pratley, Mary Pratley. The other lists Martha Maria Smith, Mary Moss alias Smith, Charlotte Moss, Ann Susan Moss, Fanny Honeybone, Ann Moss, Rebecca Smith, Lavinia [later known as Levia] Dring. These are the sixteen women who went to prison. Five of the names—Amelia, Jane and Ann Susan Moss, Elizabeth Pratley and young Mary Moss (alias Smith)—were not on the original seat. I was delighted to be able to help those in charge of the new memorial to establish that these names do now accurately identify all of the women. The fourth side carries the words, 'And those who supported them: Jane Pratley, Celia Honeybone, Elizabeth Honeybone, Eliza Honeybone, Mrs Caleb Moss.'

In finding their story, I discovered that most of the newspaper reports and articles written about the women portrayed them as a homogeneous group. I wanted to find out more about each individual woman and her life experiences, and to see if and how the women were related to each other.

The two 1873 charge sheets[2] recorded each woman's name and sentence. On the back of the charge sheets was each woman's age, marital status, place of birth, place of residence, occupation and religious affiliation. Apart from the charge sheets, my main sources of information were the transcripts of parish registers and census returns, held in the Centre for Oxfordshire Studies in the Oxford Central Library. Microfiches of the parish registers in the villages where the women were born were supplied by the Oxfordshire Family History Society. More recently I have been able to check details in census records through the website ancestry.com.

From the parish registers I was able to ascertain dates and places for their baptisms, marriages, and burials, and to see who their parents and grandparents were, whom they married, and who their husbands' parents were. I was also able to identify their brothers, sisters, and children.

The 1871 census for England was useful to establish who was living with the women in their homes, and whether the women were close neighbours or not. It also showed whether their siblings were living in the village at that time. The census allowed me to confirm the information about where the women were born, as recorded on the charge sheets. It did not give the women's occupations, but did provide those of their husbands, fathers, brothers, and sons. I went on to look up all the censuses from 1841 through to 1901 to follow their living situations, occupations, and whether they stayed in, or moved away from, the village.

The women had only five surnames between them: Dring, Honeybone, Moss, Pratley, and Smith. These were common names in the area. Some of the women's Christian names were the same: for example, there were three Marys and two Marthas. The names of the other women were also in common use: Amelia, Ann, Caroline, Charlotte, Elizabeth, Ellen, Fanny, Jane, Levia, and Susannah. Their husbands and fathers had twelve Christian names among them, all of them common at that time: Caleb, Charles, Frederick, Eli, Thomas, James, Robert, Joseph, Alfred, George (2), John (3), and William (2).

As eight of the women's surnames were Moss, it would not have been surprising if they were related, but that was not necessarily so. Two of the women whose maiden names were Moss married men surnamed Moss, yet neither was closely related to her husband. Two distinct families of Mosses lived in Ascott-under-Wychwood at that time. Going back two generations, one family descended from William Moss and Susannah Scarsebrook, while

INTRODUCTION

the other descended from George Moss and Elizabeth (Betty) Thornett. No connection has been found between William and George.

There were two sets of sisters: Jane Moss and Fanny Honeybone, and Amelia and Charlotte Moss. Several of the women were related by marriage. All worked for pay: seven were field labourers outside the home, and eight were gloveresses, usually in their homes. Young Mary Moss was employed as a servant. They all knew each other through attending either the Baptist and Methodist Chapels, or the Church of England. The village was only a mile long, with the cottages generally sitting side by side, so they would also have been neighbours.

A brief biography for each of the women named on the two charge sheets is found at the end of this book.

CHAPTER 1: VILLAGE LIFE

ASCOTT-UNDER-WYCHWOOD

The year was 1873. Queen Victoria was on the throne and William Gladstone was the Liberal Prime Minister. In the Oxfordshire village of Ascott-under-Wychwood, a small revolution was taking place. Agricultural labourers were on strike.

The village was the home of my great-great-grandparents, Jemima Moss and William Pratley. William worked as a woodman, a butcher and an agricultural labourer. Jemima, who was 58 in 1873, was a charwoman according to the 1871 census. Their son Eli and his second wife, Jane, were my great-grandparents. Two of Jemima's daughters-in-law, Mary Pratley and Elizabeth Pratley, were among the sixteen women who take centre stage in this book.

Ascott-under-Wychwood had always been an agricultural village. The 1871 census described it as consisting of '1,769 acres, one rood, and five perches of cultivated land, principally arable, and a population, according to the last (1871) census, of 462, two thirds of which are agricultural labourers and their families...'[1]

There were eight farmsteads, where Robert Hambidge, William Lardner, John Chaundy, William Venvill, Anthony Townsend, Richard Hyatt, Henry Hopkins, and Thomas Holyfield lived with their families. They were part of the system whereby such farmers were tenants of landed gentry or nobles; the tenant farmers, in turn, rented accommodation to local agricultural workers who worked the farmers' fields for wages. When Archibald Forbes, a newspaper correspondent, visited Ascott in the spring of 1873, he thought the farms in and around the village were quite large:

> From the eminence you mount when passing by Earl Ducie's estate (in Sarsden) towards Ascott, a grand view of an English pastoral scenery is spread out. The Great Western

Railway runs through the valley and from it the land rises in gentle undulations until merged in the Cotswold Hills. At this season of the year the eye delights to feast upon these verdant spaces and bright woodlands ... [they] were striking.[2]

The valley Forbes mentions is the Evenlode valley, where the village of Ascott-under-Wychwood is situated. It is on the eastern edge of the Cotswolds, midway between the market towns of Burford to the south and Chipping Norton to the north. In the 1870s, the valley was known for its deciduous woodland and fertile farmland.[3] About a mile long, the village developed from two ancient settlements, each with a castle site. The southern half was Ascott Earl, named after the Earl of Worcester.[4] The northern part was known as Ascott d'Oyley. This name came from the family of Wido de Oileio, a Norman noble who accompanied William the Conqueror when he invaded England in 1066.[5] In 1873 much of the village and land was owned by Lord Churchill,[6] the 7th Duke of Marlborough.[7]

Although described as part of the 'old' royal forest, this didn't mean Ascott was surrounded by woodland, but that it was once subject to the special forest laws. In the nineteenth century, much of this area was opened up, and the forest laws were discontinued. This made a great deal of difference to the foresters who lived there, because they had derived much of their livelihood under the old law.[8] The Disafforestation of Wychwood Forest Act, passed in 1853, saw large tracts of forest cleared. Three years later, a network of roads began to be laid out; this work was completed between October 1856 and January 1858.[9]

There were about 90 cottages in the village in 1873, a forge where William White was the blacksmith, and a recently built school; William Lee was the schoolmaster and his wife, Mary, the sewing mistress. The village green was close to the school, with a road dividing it from the schoolyard. The local hunt used to meet two or three times a year on the green with their foxhounds.

The Churchill Arms and the Swan Inn were public houses. Stage coaches from Worcester to London used to stop at the old Churchill Arms to change the horses. When the railway came in the 1840s, a new Churchill Arms was built near the level crossing.[10] In 1871 Jonathan Honey, a railway booking constable, and his young family lived in the railway station building. John Morris was the innkeeper of the Churchill Arms, and lived there with his wife, Hannah, his nephew Joseph, who was the groom and room servant,

Wychwood Forest.

and Fanny Honeybone, a cousin by marriage of Martha Smith, was the domestic servant. By 1873, Fanny had left the Churchill Arms and was working as a gloveress.

The other public house, the Swan Inn, was more centrally located. Not only did it provide a place for villagers to gather and enjoy a glass or two of beer or cider, but it also baked and sold bread. When villagers were lucky enough to obtain fresh meat, it would be roasted in the inn's large oven for them. Between 1871 and 1875 William Perkins, a baker, was the licensee of the Swan Inn.[11]

Charles Weaver and Thomas Jackson, boot and shoemakers, had a cobbler's shop as did Richard Moss, a shoemaker. There was also a small grocer's shop and a coal business.

A Baptist chapel and the twelfth-century Church of the Holy Trinity saw to the pastoral care of the parishioners and tried to uphold public morality. Reverend Robert Tweed (45) was the Vicar of Ascott. A widower, his wife Penelope having died a few years earlier, he lived with his sister Sophia (34) and their servants Charlotte Walker and Harriet Evans at the vicarage, which was reached by a driveway off London Lane. Further along the drive, beyond the vicarage, were the outbuildings, carriage house, and stables. The sides of the drive were lined with a grass verge, sheltering box trees, laurels, and other decorative shrubs and flowers. Springs in the vicarage grounds provided the main water supply for the village.[12]

By the time Harry Honeybone, nephew of Jane Moss (née Honeybone), moved to Ascott-under-Wychwood in 1876, the Reverend Samuel York, who replaced Reverend Tweed, was living in the vicarage with his wife, Frances; their housekeeper, Harriet Larch; and their cook, Ellen Coggins. Harry described Reverend York as a 'slim, genteel, slender sort of individual, and his wife one of those thick-set stodgy creatures'.[13] Harry's recollections shed light on the vicar's standing. York periodically visited the school (which was run by the Church of England). As soon as he entered the room, the pupils stood; the boys bowed and the girls curtsied. If they passed him or Mrs York in the street, they had to do the same. If they did not, they would receive 'weals on our hands from the master's cane, especially those who attended Sunday School at the Baptist Chapel'.[14]

Many of my forebears were baptised and married in the Church of the Holy Trinity. My great-great-grandmother, Jemima Moss, was baptised there, as was her father William Moss, and her grandparents George Moss and Betty Thornett. Jemima's mother, Jane, was from the village of Leafield, about five miles away. Jane's maiden name was Pratley, but she was not related to Jemima's husband, William Pratley. Jemima was William's second wife, and stepmother to Hannah and John.[15] Jemima and William would have two daughters, Mary and Sarah Lucy, and six sons, William, Frederick, Eli, Philip, Charles, and James. Frederick's and Eli's wives, Mary Pratley (née Panting) and Elizabeth Pratley (née Osman) were among the sixteen women who were imprisoned.

The church had five wooden pews at the back for the old and sick to sit on during services. Everyone else stood. Both the church and its graveyard, on higher ground than the rest of the village, were partly hidden by the stone-wall boundary lined by horse chestnut trees (removed in the early 1950s). Newly planted lime trees formed an avenue alongside the church from Church View (once called Charity Row) to the church itself. Many years later, Mrs Gwen Morgan remembered how 'the lime trees ... gave such a sweet scent in the spring and attracted so many bees ...'[16] Many shallow-rooted elm trees, at about 10-yard intervals, lined the roadsides leading into and out of the village. These trees provided firewood after strong winds broke off branches or blew down a tree or two.[17]

The Evenlode River flowed close by the low-lying village. When it rained persistently and heavily, the river overflowed its banks into the southwest end of the village, blocking any attempt to take the road leading to the nearby villages of Milton and Shipton. At the other end of the village, the road became impassable when the river flooded and turned the low-lying fields into a lake. When the temperatures dropped low enough, this lake would freeze over. One year the river itself froze, forming an ice rink where the villagers could skate or slide. At times the village was snowed in, isolating the villagers until gangs of men with shovels cleared the roads. Sometimes the walls and hedges were buried so deeply in the frozen snow that men could take their horses and carts anywhere across the country over the top.[18]

THE COTTAGES

Harry Honeybone remembered living with his grandmother, Jane Honeybone (mother of Fanny Honeybone and Jane Moss, who were later imprisoned) in an oblong thatched cottage that stood alone, with doors front and back, facing west at the far end of the village. Most of the cottages in the village were similar, all with their gardens and necessary outbuildings.

Inside, a third of the south end was divided off by a wooden partition, used as a scullery and pantry. At the north end was a fireplace, which consisted of a few bricks built up with short iron bars as crosspieces to hold them and to keep the hot embers in. The fireplace was wide, with a recess at one side where two people could sit side by side and look up through the chimney at the stars at night or the blue sky during the day. Swallows and starlings built their nests and reared their young in that broad chimney, as well as in the thatch during the summer months. In winter the rain and snow sent soot down the chimney.

A large chain hung above the fire, with hooks for hanging a kettle or pot for cooking the potatoes, cabbage or other green vegetables, and a piece of bacon or ham, all put in a net to boil. Sometimes a savoury pudding or a sweet one, consisting of treacle, jam, apple or other fruit in season, would be steamed in the pot. Most of the year sides of salted and cured pork, known as flitches, as well as hams and shoulders of bacon, were suspended inside the chimney, just above the fire, to dry or smoke. Many people did not have such a chimney in their cottages, so they used the Honeybone's to dry their meat after it was salted.

On the right of the fireplace, built into the wall, was a large oven, big enough to hold 20 loaves of bread. This used to be heated with faggots (bundles of wood 4 feet long and 12 to 15 inches wide). The faggots would be set alight in the oven, with the smoke going up the chimney; when the oven was judged to be hot enough, it would be cleaned out and the bread put in to bake. This did not happen very often, as most of the village bread was baked at the Swan Inn. On the other side of the fireplace, a staircase led up to the bedrooms. The far bedroom was reached by first passing through the nearer ones.

Attached to the house was a good-sized garden with apple, plum, and damson trees, as well as gooseberry and currant bushes. In the farthest corner was a pigsty, a wood shed, and a privy, with its earth-and-ash midden. Villagers raised one or more pigs during the year. As a rule, one was sold to pay the rent, about 50 shillings a year; the other was kept for their own use. If there was a grocer's bill or any other bill, then usually half of that pig paid this and the other half was kept to eat.

In a newspaper report (after the women's imprisonment), the tenant farmers claimed that their workers' families were generally happy and contented: 'With two exceptions the cottages and gardens are good, the rents low, and the allotments close to the village and the general condition of the labouring poor are above average of that class.' However, there was '... a large old building erected in the time of Queen Elizabeth for a village workhouse which has become a lodging-house for two classes of the labouring poor, those who would not pay more than 6d or 1s per week for rent, and those who were so objectionable as tenants, that owners refuse to receive them ...'[19]

A view put forward by Jennie Kitteringham in 'Country work girls in nineteenth-century England'[20] was that:

> the Victorian middle class used their own ideals as a yardstick to measure the failings of their inferiors. Theirs was the epitome of a 'moral' existence; and anything different from it was thought to be immoral or a symptom of immoralities to come... living in close quarters doesn't make people immoral, any more than living in a country house or a vicarage kept their betters chaste... living so much on top of one another — as did the labourer's family — meant that adults and children were used to living together.[21]

Christopher Holloway was the chairman of the Oxford district of the National Agricultural Labourers' Union and based in Woodstock. Born in Wootton, he worked as an agricultural labourer and was a Methodist lay preacher.[22] He also visited the village in 1873. He described the living conditions of the farm labourers' homes he saw (perhaps the 'two exceptions' noted earlier by the farmers) as

> very bad indeed... Imagine a narrow place, like a coal cellar, down which you go two or three steps, no flooring except broken stones, no ceiling, no grate, rough walls, a bare ladder leading to the one narrow bedroom about six feet wide, containing two double bedsteads for a man his wife and three young children...[23]

This was the bedroom of Elizabeth Pratley (one of the sixteen women imprisoned), and her husband Eli, their two daughters, four-year-old Elizabeth and two-year-old Ellen, and their baby son, nine-month-old Eli.[24] Holloway wrote:

> The whole place was as wretchedly bad and miserable as imagination can conceive, and only divided by a rough wooden partition not reaching the roof, but over which you may look into the bedroom of the next adjoining house, equally wretched and miserable...[25]

In that bedroom slept Eli's brother, Frederick Pratley, his wife Mary (another of the sixteen women who were imprisoned), and their six children: George

ASCOTT-UNDER-WYCHWOOD

The dwellings along Charity Row, now Church View, where some of the women lived.
(People's History Museum, Manchester, UK.)

Frederick (10), Frederick James (8), John William (6), Charles Ernest (4), Mary Ann (2) and baby Thomas, who was just a few weeks old. To get to their bedroom, they had to go through the first bedroom.[26]

Until recently a third dwelling, one room down and one up, had been occupied by a man, his wife, and their six children, 'whose only way to bed was through the bedroom No. 2 as No. 3 had no staircase or ladder or any other way of access to the bedroom'.[27]

Another cottage with one room down and one room up was occupied by Thomas Moss and his family. Thomas was a carter and a timber hauler.[28] He lived with his wife Eliza and four children, George (10), Jane (3), and Eliza's two older girls: Mary aged 17 (one of the women imprisoned) and Emily (22).

The Elizabethan workhouse across the road from the Swan Inn where Elizabeth and Mary Pratley lived with their families.
(People's History Museum, Manchester, UK.)

CHAPTER 2: WORKING LIFE

GLOVING, DOMESTIC SERVICE, and FARMING

As well as being responsible for the well-being of their families, village women worked extremely hard to bring extra money into the household. Of the sixteen women who went to prison, one (young Mary Moss) was a servant and seven worked as farm labourers. The other eight worked as gloveresses.

GLOVING

The leather glove-making trade employed considerable numbers in the Wychwood area, because the raw materials in the form of animal skins were obtainable close by. Glove-making was concentrated in villages such as Ascott-under-Wychwood, on the edge of the Wychwood Forest.

The Woodstock and Charlbury[1] glove factories prepared the animal skins: generally deer or sheep. The skins were tanned, sorted, dyed and finished before they were cut into rectangles.[2] A slitter or webber would then use steel punches or 'webs' to cut the leather into the twenty components which made up a pair of gloves. These components—four hand-with-fingers shapes, twelve fourchettes (the pieces between the fingers), and four thumb shapes—were delivered to the women. Usually they were dispatched in bundles of three, six, or twelve pairs, each with the requisite matching sewing thread.[3] The women 'did the gloving'[4] inside the home, or outside the door if the weather was sunny and warm. They sewed the pieces together by hand, earning between fourpence and fivepence a pair. A good gloveress could make up to three pairs in a day, earning between five shillings and seven shillings a week.[5] According

Women's work — gloving.

to Muriel Groves, the women would often meet in each other's homes and talk as they worked, and in cold weather they would warm their feet around a large ash-pan.[6]

Gloving was a viable alternative to being a servant. George Hambidge, from nearby Leafield, born in 1840, remembered that young women who made gloves very seldom went into service. A Wootton gloveress told the 1867 Royal Commission of Inquiry into Trade Unions that 'a girl ought to be 14 or 15 before she is trusted with a glove'.[7] Of the eight Ascott martyrs who were gloveresses, Caroline Moss must have moved back home to help her sister, Harriet, with her gloving. Levia Dring had four daughters living at home, three of whom were gloving with their mother; the youngest, Alice, was still at school in 1871. The other gloveresses, Ellen Pratley and Martha, Amelia, Jane and Mary Moss, did not have daughters who were old enough to help with the gloving.

In 1871 Sarah Surmer, from another Oxfordshire village, recounted how she 'took the bundles of completed gloves into Woodstock by the weekly wagon, and brought back supplies of raw materials'.[8] Doris Warner, who lived in Ascott-under-Wychwood, remembered how several women brought their bundles of gloves, tied up in red and white handkerchiefs (known locally as bundling hankechers), to her father's shop to be called for by the carrier's cart. This cart went from Leafield to Chipping Norton twice a week.[9]

FARMING

Most of the men in the village, and some of the women, worked as agricultural labourers, employed by the tenant farmers, who rented their land from the landowners. Robert Hambidge was the tenant of Crown Farm, the largest in the village, with 400 acres. It was one of the farms created following the 1853 Act of Parliament for the disafforestation of Wychwood, which enabled Crown Farm and others to be developed after a further area of woodland was cleared.[10] On the farm there were twelve Shire horses, making up three and sometimes four teams that worked in single file. Hambidge also owned one or two hunters and carriage horses. Four bullocks worked in a team in single file. He had seven or eight milking cows, twenty or thirty steers and heifers, a 'superior' flock of 500 sheep, and young stock, as well as a number of pigs and hundreds of poultry, including fowls, turkeys, ducks, geese, and guinea fowl, along with dogs and several beehives.[11]

Robert Hambidge was a relative newcomer to the village, having previously farmed 169 acres in Westcote in Gloucestershire, about five miles away. He was born in Icomb, not far from Westcote, and his wife, Rose, was born in the neighbouring village of Rissington. From these villages, situated higher on the Cotswold Hills, they would have been able to see Ascott-under-Wychwood nestled in the Evenlode valley.

Robert's workers and their families had lived in and around the Ascott-under-Wychwood area for many generations. They belonged to the woodlands of Wychwood, knew everybody, and they or their fathers had helped to clear the forest. Now they worked the land.

The winter months were usually cold and miserable, with rain, fog, snow, and wind. Harry Honeybone had boyhood memories of working in the rain on Crown Farm:

> I can remember the second horseman getting wet through one day. He went home to change or dry his clothes because there were not many people who had a change of

The house of tenant farmer Robert Hambidge, on whose property the strike began.
(People's History Museum, Manchester, UK.)

clothing. He was a little longer than the gaffer thought he ought to be. I believe his wages were only 9 shillings a week, so the farmer said, 'I will drop his wages 1 shilling per week then perhaps he will be able to buy a top coat.'

We had to stick it in all kinds of weather... We used to get wet through and then go home. One day it rained and snowed all day and we stuck it. I had to because the men did, water was running down my legs and into my boots. When I got home, Grandmother was out at the mill, there was no fire. ... I had to make a fire, then I was walking around the bedroom in my birthday suit looking for a dry shirt and stockings to put on. I had to dry my clothes as best I could, then get back to do my work. This is only one of many instances.[12]

When it was too wet to work with the horses in the fields, Harry remembered:

being set to do odd jobs about the farmstead but nearly always as soon as the household was aroused and out and about. It used to be the cowman's job every morning to waken the Master. He used to call, 'Master, Master', until there was a response. Then the keys were let down on a piece of string to unlock the various establishments. As soon as breakfast was over, when they knew I was not in the fields, they used to send for me into the kitchen. There they would plonk about twenty pairs of boots and shoes all covered with soil and dirt of all descriptions... I made them shine with old fashioned Martin's blacking so well that one day someone opened their purse string and sent me in the large tip of two pence... In addition to boot cleaning there was coal to get, wood to chop and all the necessary drudgery work about the home...[13]

Women also worked in the fields, and helped bring in more money as best they could. As mentioned, seven of the sixteen women who were later imprisoned were farm labourers. Their work was valued mainly because, like the boys, they could fill the place of a man at lower wages, and could be depended on. Boys received from four shillings upwards a week (or eightpence a day) and women nine- to tenpence a day.[14] In winter and spring they hacked the turnips, which had been half-eaten by the sheep, up out of the ground.[15] They filled dung carts and spread the manure onto the fields. Their work also included stone picking, peeling willow twigs used in making baskets, and pea picking.[16]

Later in the year they cleared the weeds from the wheat and barley fields and the pastures. They cut up thistles and other noxious plants with their small narrow spades. In late summer their tasks were mostly concerned with haymaking.[17] Commonly used plants for hay included mixtures of grasses such as ryegrass as well as legumes such as sainfoin, alfalfa (lucerne), and red, white, and subterranean clovers. After the hay was cut and dried, the women would rake it up into rows, and turn it with pitchforks. Once the hay was rowed up and dry, the women would toss it loose with their pitchforks onto a horse-drawn cart or wagon.[18]

Harvest time was even busier. When the crops of wheat, barley, and oats were cut by the men with either scythes, sickles or bagging hooks, the women, and often the children, followed to help rake, bind, and stook the sheaves.[19] The women would also stand on the rick or haystack to hand up the sheaves.[20]

Jennie Kitteringham writes in 'Country work girls in nineteenth-century England':[21]

> The [female] field worker was anathema to the middle class, the complete opposite to what they expected in their own women — helplessness. But wages paid to the farm labourer were too low for him to be the sole provider of his family; women and children had to sell their own labour, too, in order to survive. Women were forced out of the isolation of the home into the society of the field... their work role was in conflict with the moral one prescribed for them. They were too independent, too free.[22]

Women's work in the field.
(*OXFORDSHIRE of One Hundred Years Ago*, Eleanor Chance)

GLOVING, DOMESTIC SERVICE, and FARMING

The winter of 1872 was wetter than usual.[23] The men would not have been able to hoe the beans or turnips, or sow new crops, because the soil became unworkable in the wet weather. No work meant no money. The warmest and most congenial places for the labourers were the nearby public houses, the Churchill Arms and the Swan Inn, both an easy walk from their homes. Around the fireplaces with their burning logs and glowing embers, the men would be able to escape their homes, relax with their ales, and commiserate with each other about their conditions of living.

Like the men, the women labourers could not work the fields in this wettest of seasons. They could not do much inside either, as their miserable homes were not suitable for sitting down and gloving. It was hard work sweeping a dirt floor covered with broken stones. There was no running water, electricity or proper sanitation. Without even a grate on the fire, their meals were simple, although they enjoyed drinking tea, milk, beer, and broth, as well as eating meat and bread.[24]

FALLING FOUL of the LAW

Of the sixteen women who became known as the Ascott martyrs, three were Pratleys.

Some members of the wider Pratley family were well known to the two local magistrates, who would later preside over the women's trial. The Reverend Harris and the Reverend Carter had been involved in convicting and sentencing three of the Pratley men for various offences. These men were John and his half-brothers, William and Eli, three of the seven sons of my great-great-grandfather, William Pratley. Their history sheds light on the various ways in which farm labourers could fall foul of the law.

In 1858 John Pratley, the father of five children, had been sentenced to four months' imprisonment with hard labour for assaulting his wife, Jane, with intent to do her bodily harm. He said in defence that she had 'given him great provocation'. John had been remanded twice because Jane was too ill to attend the court. This happened one month after their three-month-old baby daughter, Emma, died.[25]

In 1866 John, by then the father of nine children, appeared before Reverend Harris, Lord Churchill, and J. H. Worsley for stealing a peck and a half of apples from his master, John Venville, one of the tenant farmers. He was convicted and again sent to prison for six weeks with hard labour.

Alcohol was a factor in some of the Pratley convictions. Joseph Arch, who would become president of the National Agricultural Labourers' Union, wrote about the disturbing practice of the men being given alcohol instead of wages:

> Perhaps one of the greatest evils which affect the condition of the labourer... is the practice of giving beer or cider to the men in lieu of wages. This custom not only prevents a fair share of the wages going for the support of the family, but generates that love of drink which... is the curse of the labourer.[26]

John's younger half-brother, William, seems to have had a drinking problem and a tendency towards violence. Between February 1861 and August 1866, he was convicted for being 'drunk and riotous' six times—once in Ascott, twice in Leafield, and three times in Shipton. Each time he appeared before the Reverend Harris, and on four of these occasions before the Reverend Carter as well. In most cases William was fined a sum of money including costs. Twice he could not afford the fines and was sent to prison instead, once for a week and once for six weeks with hard labour.

William's younger brother Eli also got into trouble with the law. In 1866 Eli had assaulted William Brooks of Ascott, by striking him on the head. He appeared before Reverend Harris, B. J. Whippy, J. H. Worsley, and R. S. Baker, and was fined £2 including costs.[27] Two years later, in 1868, Eli was found 'drunk and riotous' at Shipton. On 29 April he appeared before the Reverends Harris and Carter and R. L. Baker, and was fined ten shillings, including costs.

Eli married Ann Elizabeth Osman (known as Elizabeth[28]) in March 1869, and their baby daughter Elizabeth was baptised soon after on 4 June. Early the next year Eli was back before the Reverends Harris and Carter. This time he was charged by William Lardner, another tenant farmer of Ascott, with stealing forty pounds of flesh from a dead calf, valued at three shillings, on 25 January. It appeared that Lardner had cut up and dressed a dead steer for his dogs. Eli asked him for some meat, and Lardner gave him two joints. Later, two legs of the meat were found in Eli's house by Police Constable Smith. Eli explained that he did not know which meat Mr Lardner had intended him to take, and so he took what he wanted. But he was sent to prison for a month with hard labour.[29]

CHAPTER 3: THE UNION
'DISRESPECTFUL, VEXATIOUS, and RIOTOUS'

According to seven of its tenant farmers, Ascott-under-Wychwood was on the whole a 'peaceful and orderly place...'[1] until the Agricultural Labourers' Union arrived in 1872, causing the farm workers they employed to become 'disrespectful, vexatious, and riotous'. Farmers who did not agree with the union principles were said to be greeted with 'Baa, Baa, Black legs; old black legs, baa, baa, baa.'[2]

The 1871 Trades Union Act had permitted the formation of unions; but the Criminal Law Amendment Act, passed the same day, forbade anyone to stop workers entering their workplace. In effect, it prevented striking workers from picketing. A meeting of labourers, chaired by Joseph Arch, was held at the Stag's Head Inn, in Wellesbourne, Warwickshire, on 7 February 1872. Within days of that meeting the labourers of Leek Wootton, near Warwick, 'drew up a list of demands for higher wages, the introduction of overtime rates, an eleven-hour day and extra pay for Sunday work, and resolved to strike if their claim was rejected'. Arch urged the men to aim for 'payments for members on official strike or locked out by employers, and help during times of sickness and infirmity, so as to prevent pauperism'.[3]

Although many women also worked as farm labourers, or, as they were usually called, field workers, they were not permitted to join the union. One reason for this was that Joseph Arch condemned the employment of women in agriculture. He was opposed on principle to women working for pay outside the home. He emphasised that 'Wives must be at home, and the father must earn wages sufficient to maintain the family comfortably.'[4] It was believed that women working out in the fields all day were more likely to neglect their homes and families; but the union was also concerned that women would compete with the male workers and drag down male wages.

Arch was a Methodist preacher and had been an agricultural labourer himself, as well as a champion hedger and ditcher. He agreed to chair the Wellesbourne meeting because he knew the conditions of these men and their families. When he arrived at the Stag's Head Inn, such a large group, estimated at between 600 and 2,000, met him that they had to move to the village green. He stood on a pig stool under the old chestnut tree to speak to them. The winter evening was damp, cold, and dark, but the men hung lanterns on beanpoles. Arch later recorded in his autobiography:

> When I reached Wellesbourne, lo, and behold, it was as lively as a swarm of bees in June. We settled that I should address the meeting under the old chestnut tree; and I expected to find some thirty or forty of the principal men there. What then was my surprise to see not a few tens but many hundreds of labourers assembled; there were nearly two thousand of them. The news that I was going to speak that night had been spread about; and so the men had come in from all the villages round within a radius of 10 miles. Not a circular had been sent out nor a handbill printed, but from cottage to cottage, and from farm to farm, the word had been passed on; and here were the labourers gathered together in their hundreds...
>
> These white slaves of England stood there with the darkness all about them, like the children of Israel waiting for someone to lead them out of the land of Egypt...[5]

Arch was also concerned for the next generation. He was opposed to labourers' children being employed on farms. He wanted better education for them, and this could not happen if they had to work to make ends meet. The labourers knew that their children needed education, as well as food and clothing, and sent them to the village school as often as possible; but to help the family, children were sent off to work when it was available, even if it was only to scare away crows. Often their education ceased at a young age, because of the need to bring in more money. In 1881, ten-year-old Harry Honeybone had to leave school after he had successfully passed the sixth standard, and go to work on Crown Farm for Robert Hambidge.[6]

Much of the information regarding the principles of unionism and notices of meetings was spread to the labourers by word of mouth. It was also spread in songs that became popular. John Tymms (later Timms),[7] born in Ascott-under-Wychwood and a young boy in the 1870s, remembered that he was playing marbles with his friends one day when they heard a man singing about unionism. He sang a verse of his song, and then the chorus, and the chorus was repeated so often that John remembered it fifty years later:

> Oh, come and join our Unionhood,
> For we are bound to do you good,
> Oh, come and join each heart and hand,
> Oh, come and join our Union band.[8]

The meeting in Wellesbourne heralded the start of the Warwickshire Agricultural Labourers' Union. With its low and affordable subscription of 'tuppence' (2d) a week, it thrived and membership grew rapidly.[9]

Two months after Joseph Arch spoke in Wellesbourne, the Ascott women may have encouraged their menfolk to attend the first meeting of the union in the Oxford district. It was held on the Milton Recreation Ground in Milton-under-Wychwood on 16 April 1872, a mile and a half from Ascott. At the Milton meeting, the rules were read and, after some discussion, fifty labourers became members. The secretary was Joseph Leggett, a carpenter from Milton-under-Wychwood.[10]

It seems likely that many of the agricultural labourers from the nearby village of Ascott-under-Wychwood would have walked the mile and a half to attend that first meeting, which may have begun, as they often did, with the song setting the tone for working together:

> Welcome to our meeting
> Friends and strangers, old and young,
> Farmers, tradesmen, labourers greeting,
> Every hand and eye and tongue,
> Every name today is Brother;
> All our creed is love each other.'[11]

The working conditions of the labourers and their change of attitude after joining the union were reflected in many songs written around that time. 'The Fine Old English Labourer' would have been sung after the introductory speech.[12]

> Come boys, and listen to my song, a song of honest toil,
> 'Tis of the English labourer, the tiller of the soil;
> I'll tell you how he used to fare, and all the ills he bore,
> Till he stood up in his manhood, resolved to bear no more.
> This fine old English labourer, one of the present time.

He used to take whatever wage the farmer chose to pay,
And work as hard as any horse for eighteen pence a day;
Or if he grumbled at the nine he dared to ask for ten,
The angry farmer cursed and swore, and sacked him there and then.
This fine old English labourer, one of the present time.

They used to treat them as they liked in the evil days of old,
They thought there was no power on earth to beat the power of Gold,
They used to threaten what they'd do whenever work was slack,
But now he laughs their threats to scorn with the Union at his back.
This fine old English labourer, one of the present time.[13]

Joseph Arch convinced the labourers that their work of tilling the soil was important and necessary. They worked in all weathers and long hours at the behest of their employers. Until the union arrived, they were paid a wage of eighteen pence a day, or nine shillings a week, and if they complained they were liable to be sacked. Their breakfast consisted of a crust or two of bread in the morning before they set off to work, and they dined on potatoes, with a lump of bacon if they were lucky. When the labourer walked along the fields he could often see rabbits 'devouring his master's growing crops',[14] but he was not allowed to catch them because it was part of his master's sport to go rabbit shooting. If the keeper found him with a rabbit or a wire to catch a rabbit, he would be taken to court and punished by the magistrates, who were usually the local parson and the squire.

Through the union, as Arch would have explained, the labourers could join together to demand a fair wage, because the land would be of no use if their labour was not available, and it was time that they had their proper share of any profit. If the farmer or squire did not like their demands, then they would walk off the land with union support.[15] Although the Ascott women were not allowed to become members, they may have mingled around the outer edges of the crowd.

Another public meeting was held on 25 April 1872 on the Recreation Ground in nearby Shipton-under-Wychwood. The meeting was chaired by Charles Cox, a farm labourer, who at 31 years old was the youngest member of the committee. After the rules were read to the assembled crowd, a large number joined the union from different parishes.[16]

The committee met again a few days later on 29 April, with further meetings in May. At the first monthly delegate meeting, held on 23 May,

Eli Robinson was the delegate from Ascott-under-Wychwood. Also present were delegates from other West Oxfordshire villages, including Milton, Shipton, Lineham, Westcote, Taynton, Fulbrook, Swinbrook, Kingham, Burford, Minster, Asthall, Leafield, and Bledington.[17]

These meetings led to the establishment of the National Agricultural Labourers' Union in Leamington on 29 May 1872, with Joseph Arch as its chairman.[18] Henry Taylor, a Leamington carpenter, was appointed paid secretary, and Mathew Vincent, proprietor of the *Royal Leamington Chronicle*, which had always supported the labourers' cause, became the voluntary secretary.[19] Twenty-six counties were represented.

> The conference bore a strong resemblance to a religious revival, which is not surprising, since many of the delegates owed their presence at Leamington to their training as Methodist preachers. Speeches were punctuated with cries of 'Amen', 'Praise Him', and other devout utterances. One delegate said, 'Sir, this be a blessed day: this 'ere Union be the Moses to lead us poor men up out o' Egypt.'[20]

The union's main aim at that time was to obtain an increase in male wages and to limit their working day to nine hours, with extra payment for overtime and Sunday working.[21]

Emigration was seen as another possible solution to the labourers' problem of how to better their lives. In 1872 a letter was sent to the New Zealand government, signed by Joseph Arch, Chairman; Henry Taylor, Secretary; Reverend Frederick Attenborough, Congregational Pastor and Treasurer of the Warwickshire Labourers' Union,[22] and all members of the Committee of the National Agricultural Labourers' Union. It requested 'free passages from an English port if not from their homes be provided for all eligible labourers and their families who are willing to seek your shores; and further that provision be made for their reception and for their transfer to fields in which their labour may be most in demand.'[23]

CHAPTER 4: ON STRIKE
FARM LABOURERS UNITE

The formation of the National Agricultural Labourers' Union in the winter of 1872 quickly brought hope of better things to come. The men's wages rose from nine shillings to twelve shillings a week, but this was still hardly enough to feed their ever-growing families. In spring 1873, the union decided to go for a further increase of two shillings a week for the labourers on Crown Farm, undoubtedly because it was the biggest in the district.

The women would have been pleased when their husbands, fathers, and brothers brought home their wages on the evening of Saturday 12 April. Robert Hambidge, who employed some of these men, was later reported to have given each of them twelve shillings on 'good and friendly terms'.[1]

Sometime between receiving their wages on Saturday evening, and going to work on Monday morning, Hambidge's labourers must have attended a union meeting. It would have been at this meeting that the union told the men to ask for another two shillings a week. When they turned up for work on Monday morning, the men informed Hambidge that they wanted two shillings a week more, and if he refused they would stop work until he agreed to the increase.

Hambidge probably wondered what the world was coming to, like the farmer who later told Archibald Forbes, when he gave him a lift in his dog cart: 'That seed-time and harvest should never fail he has from boyhood stoutly held... but that these agricultural labourers should agitate and combine passes his understanding...'[2]

Hambidge refused to raise the wages for everyone, but did agree to pay his more efficient labourers the extra two shillings. Those who were not as strong and active as the others, because of their age or infirmity, would still receive twelve shillings a week, but there was, and would be, plenty of piece-work for them. The men refused these offers. They all agreed that unless everyone received the extra two shillings a week, no one would continue to work.

According to the *Oxfordshire Weekly News,* Hambidge advised them to reconsider, and think of what would be best in the long run. He said he would be glad if they would go to work on the old terms for the present, as the farm work would not get done without them, but added that he was not going to be dictated to. All the farm labourers, as well as the carters, then left the farm. 'The carters had fed and harnessed their horses and were going into the fields to drill barley. The men returned, unharnessed the horses, shut the stable door, and left the work.'[3]

The *Oxfordshire Weekly News* reported that the following week Hambidge took one of the carters, a weekly servant, to court, where charges were laid against him for leaving his work without due notice. The charge was fully proved, resulting in the carter being fined £4 12s 6d. A union delegate paid the fine and the carter returned to work. But Hambidge was left in the middle of his intended backward barley sowing, as well as having all his animals to care for, with only a head shepherd, a youth, and the carters to help.

A parish meeting was immediately called. The parochial officers, who were also the tenant farmers of the village, agreed to act in unity with the neighbouring parishes, where the large landed proprietors considered that twelve shillings a week for day labourers was a fair price, as there was continuous piece-work at a higher rate than the previous year.[4] A week later, on the morning of 21 April, all the labourers belonging to the union left their respective farms and refused to do any kind of work for their former employers.

While the farm labourers were on strike, the union paid them nine shillings a week. However, after a fortnight the union found work for them about five miles away, felling and barking timber. Evidently, some twenty men left the village each day at 5 a.m. and returned at 7 p.m. They were paid 2s 6d a day. Later, Hambidge reckoned that they could have been doing piece-work with their wives in the fields, hoeing close to their homes and earning more than double that sum.[5] After a two-week standoff, two of Hambidge's labourers returned to work.[6]

By the second week of May, the men had been on strike for four weeks, and the work that needed doing on Robert Hambidge's farm was building up. At least the carters had been able to sow the barley in time for the autumn harvest, but weeds were sprouting amongst the beans. The shepherd responsible for caring for the sheep and lambs would be able to move them to another field, as well as protect them from inclement weather, foxes, and dogs.[7] But while the turnip leaves had been eaten by the sheep, the round roots needed to be grubbed or hooked up so they could eat the remains.

It was the carters' responsibility to feed and groom the horses, as well as sow the barley seed. However, the bullocks and young stock needed to be fed, and the cows needed milking and feeding. The shepherd and a young man, both said to be yearly servants, would be able to do their share of the work, and Hambidge probably had to roll up his sleeves and do more than usual. Perhaps Hambidge's wife, Rose, and their children helped too.

Having endured four weeks of this, Robert Hambidge induced John Hodgkins and John Millin, a couple of eighteen-year-olds from Ramsden, some five miles away, to come and work for him for 7s 6d per day each.[8] One of their tasks was to hoe a field of beans. (The farmers would later claim: 'We, the occupiers of the land, had no alternative but to seek non-union labourers where we could find them.'[9])

This is where the women stepped in. Their actions were later reported in the newspaper:

> On Sunday 11th of May, [the women] were informed that two strange boys were working on Hambidge's farm, from which the Union men had retired. They discussed the matter and consulted together (the greater part of them being related to a family named Moss), and determined to wait upon the boys to represent to them the manner in which they were injuring their own order.[10]

The next day, Monday 12 May, Robert Hambidge and the other farmers left early to attend the large annual horse fair at Stow-on-the-Wold, eleven miles away in Gloucestershire.[11] That same day, the women from Ascott-under-Wychwood got together and left early also, to reach the bean field in time to ask the boys not to work for Mr Hambidge. Their purpose was to tell these youths that Hambidge's labourers were on strike, and explain that if they worked in place of the striking men, they would harm the effect of the strike. The women's simple actions were to have far-reaching consequences not only for the women themselves and their families, but also for the union, for the Liberal government of the day, and for the justice system itself.

What happened next varied according to who was telling the story. The next chapter details how it was described in the courtroom and reported in several newspapers.[12] The two youths, Hodgkins and Millin, made statements under oath to prove that they were threatened, molested, and obstructed from entering their work place. The women, also under oath, denied these claims, though they did say they had spoken to the youths and asked them not to go to work.

It seems that the Pratley women (Jane, Mary, Elizabeth, and Ellen) did not tell their menfolk about the two youths coming from Ramsden during the strike. This was not surprising: with their tendency to violence when aggravated or drunk, it was quite possible that the Pratleys would have seriously injured the strike-breakers.

When Robert Hambidge heard about the encounter between the women and the boys, it seems that he decided to make sure the women were summonsed. The following day, Tuesday, was rent day, when the clerk of the Chipping Norton justices, acting in his capacity as an agent, visited the Swan Inn to receive the rents from the tenant farmers of the Churchill Estate, including Hambidge.[13] As the *Oxfordshire Weekly News* later explained:

> Rent day is still an important day for the farmers to meet and hold sweet counsel together. Much would not be thought of the circumstance if on the day after rent day the two boys had not been conveyed by Hambidge [apparently acting on the clerk's advice] to the county justice's office in Chipping Norton. The summonses followed in due course...[14]

The Holy Trinity Church where the women met before going to the bean field.

The area known as 'Uffle Hollow' where the women met up with the youths.
(Peoples History Museum, Manchester, UK.)

CHAPTER 5: IN COURT

THE TRIAL of the 'AGRICULTURAL AMAZONS'

Seventeen women were summonsed. A week later, on Wednesday 21 May 1873, they travelled to Chipping Norton, to answer before the Chadlington Petty Sessions a charge of:

> unlawfully molesting and obstructing John Hodgkins and John Millin being with a view to quit their employment contrary to the Act made in the 34th and 35th years of the reign of Queen Victoria entitled 'An Act to amend the Criminal Law relating to violence, threats and molestation'.[1]

This was the 1871 Trades Union Act, which outlawed any form of picketing.

As mentioned earlier, seven of the women worked as field labourers: Martha Smith, Charlotte Moss, Ann Susan Moss, Ann Moss, Rebecca Smith, Elizabeth Pratley (married to Eli) and Mary Pratley (married to Frederick, another Pratley brother). Another eight worked as gloveresses: Martha Moss, Caroline Moss, Levia Dring, Amelia Moss, Jane Moss, Ellen Pratley,[2] Fanny Honeybone, and Mary Moss. Young Mary Moss (otherwise Smith) worked as a servant.[3] Jane Pratley[4] was charged but not convicted.

According to Doris Warner's version of events in the play she wrote in 1953, Mr Hambidge provided a couple of wagons to take the women to Chipping Norton in time for their afternoon appearance before the magistrates.[5] Mary Pratley took her six-week-old baby, Thomas, with her, and Elizabeth Pratley took her six-month-old baby, Eli. It would have taken about an hour to reach the new purpose-built police station, which sat in the triangular intersection between Banbury Road and London Road. The Superintendent, Joseph Lakin, lived on the top floor with his wife, Mary,

A wagon similar to the ones used to take the women to the Chipping Norton Police Station and the Oxford County Gaol.

The Swan Inn where the women were going to take the youths for a drink.
(Peoples History Museum, Manchester UK.)

and two daughters, Emma (12) and Sarah Ann (8). Richard Giles, a police officer, and William Alcock, a police sergeant, also lived there.[6]

The seventeen women and their two babies entered the courtroom on the ground floor of the Chipping Norton police station in the afternoon of Wednesday 21 May 1873. They sat on hard wooden benches. The clerk read out the charges. Each woman was accused of 'unlawfully molesting and obstructing John Hodgkins and John Millin, workmen in the employment of Robert Hambidge on 12 May, 1873'.

A local solicitor, Mr H. C. Wilkins, conducted the proceedings[7] before the magistrates, the Reverend Thomas Harris (chairman) and the Reverend William Edward Dickson Carter. Also present were Mr Rawlinson, the clerk of the court, and Christopher Holloway, the union representative, who would pay a fine should it be necessary, and some of the women's husbands.

John Hodgkins was called first to the stand. He said that on his way to work, together with John Millin, at about 8 o'clock in the morning of Monday 12 May, they met about thirty women, who at first were sitting down, and who asked the workmen where they were going. They replied that they were going to work. Hodgkins continued:

When we got to the field the women surrounded the gate. Martha Smith was one. She had a stick in her hand and defied us going into the field. Mary Moss also obstructed our entrance into the field. Martha Moss was not round the gate. Charlotte Moss also had a stick in her hand, and stood before the gate. I did not notice Ann Susan Moss... Fanny Honeyborn [sic] was there but she hadn't a stick. Ann Moss was there, but without a stick. Rebecca Smith was not there. Caroline Moss was there, but not before the gate. Elizabeth Pratley I did not observe, Mary Pratley was there, but not in front of the gate. Lavinia [Levia] Dring was present, but I did not see her before the gate. Amelia Moss was before the gate, Jane Moss was there. Ellen Pratley was not before the gate, neither was Mary Moss, who hadn't a stick, to the best of my belief. She wore a blue bonnet.[8]

Hodgkins went on to say that John Millin:

had a hoe stick in his hand, which one of the defendants tried to take away. The women stood before the gate, and we were afraid they would do us some injury. We went back to the farm, and the women followed. They pushed one another against us. Someone pushed Martha Smith against me, also Caroline Moss and Fanny Honeyborn. Some of them pushed me into the hedge. They said they would duck us if we went to work. Fanny Honeyborn [sic] and Martha Smith told us this. When I got to Mr Hambidge's house I told him[9] that we should leave, as the women said that the next morning the men would stop us.[10]

An hour later, Hodgkins and Millin went back to the field.

> The women met us from another route. They walked beside us, and Caroline Moss took hold of my arm. They said they would not let us work, we must join the Union. They wanted to get us to Ascott to have some drink. When I got into the hard road again I laid down, as the defendants said I should not go to work. All of the women stood round me. I stayed there about two hours, because I was afraid that if I went to work the women would do me some hurt.
>
> Afterwards I got up and went towards the farm again. When I got to a stile near Ascott, they wanted me to go into the village, but I refused. They then compelled me to go. I then met the policeman, and told him. Some of the women went away. The policeman then went back with me to my work. I was then not afraid.[11]

Hodgkins said that he knew most of the women by sight. When asked by the chairman, he was not sure that Mary Pratley was there. Each of the defendants questioned Hodgkins, but he did not change his account in any way.

In his testimony, John Millin said that he left Ramsden with John Hodgkins at a quarter to seven in the morning.

> Several women met us and asked where we were going. They said we were not to go to work as the other men had struck for higher wages, and it was not right for us to go. They told us that if we would go to Ascott they would give us as much victuals and drink as we pleased to have. They all stood round the gate of the field in which we were going to work, so that we dare not go in...[12]
>
> Martha Smith had a whip in her hand, Mary Moss had a stick. Martha Moss stood before the gate, but without a stick...[13] Ann Susan Moss was not before the gate. Fanny Honeyborn [sic] was before the gate. Rebecca Smith, Caroline Moss, Elizabeth Pratley, and Mary Pratley were there, but not before the gate. Jane Pratley I did not see.[14]

With the exception of Jane Moss, Millin recognised the remainder of the defendants as being there. He said: 'I was afraid to go into the gate fearing the women would do us some harm. We then went to Ascott, some of the defendants walked before, and others followed. I was carrying a hoe stick, one woman tried to take it away.' Millin identified Ann Susan Moss as that woman, but said that she did not succeed. 'I went to Mr Hambidge's house when I left the road, saw Hodgkins by the stile, the women were all round him. I could not hear what they said.'[15]

As Jane Pratley was not positively identified by either Hodgkins and Millin, she was accordingly discharged and left the courtroom.

Emma Wright was next called as witness for the defence. She declared that 'none of the defendants had either sticks or whips and that they did not molest or obstruct the men in the least'.[16] Martha Smith and several of the defendants stated 'they did not interfere with the men, but merely told them that their poor men were locked out'.[17]

After their return from prison, the women told a reporter who interviewed them for the *Oxfordshire Weekly News*:

> About 21 women and several children set off to the farm. A local carpenter was met on the road...a young girl came out of the group and tried rompingly to take away his stick, which she retained afterwards as a trophy.

When Hodgkins and Millin arrived, the women greeted them with, 'Where be you agoin'?' Hodgkins replied, 'No odds to you.'[18]

The women said they had explained to the youths that they should not work on the farm, as it would harm their husbands' efforts. The youths said they were not aware there was a lockout, and they never attempted to enter the gate of the field. The women protested that not a harsh word was used and that they convinced the youths, who said they would go down to the farm, get their money and stop working for Mr Hambidge.[19]

A *Daily News* article commented later:

> women, the wives of labourers, probably field workers themselves, are not always very gentle in their walk and conversation; they express scorn or dislike with a vehemence that might discompose and even disgust Lady Clara Vere de Vere.[20] But then the two sturdy fellows so attacked were not two fine ladies, and probably considered that hard words break no bones.[21]

The women said they went down the road with Hodgkins and Millin and waited outside while the two youths went on to the house. The pair were told that Robert Hambidge had gone to the Stow Fair, so they came away and stopped in the rick yard. John Millin joined the women, who said if they weren't going to take their husbands' work away then they should be treated with 'some drink'. John Hodgkins, however, went away and was met afterwards at the junction of two footpaths where there was a stile, and where three young girls started playing about with him. Then the whole party sat on the ground and Hodgkins pelted the girls with tufts of grass. By and by one of the girls offered to help him over the stile, 'but owing to some mismanagement he tumbled over, joining in the peals of merriment which the fiasco occasioned'.[22]

The Chipping Norton Police Station.

Inside the courtroom in the Chipping Norton Police Station, which became the billiard room in more recent times. In 2015 it closed as a police station.

THE TRIAL of the 'AGRICULTURAL AMAZONS'

According to another newspaper report, 'Hambidge's wife despatched a messenger for a policeman... to escort the young men to their work, and the body of women accompanied him; beguiling the way with friendly conversation, and ultimately returning some distance down the road with him.'[23]

The *Daily News* suggests that 'Not a blow was struck; on the appearance of one policeman the gang of agricultural Amazons made good their retreat, and, under the sufficient shield of one constable's baton, the 'molested' rustics tranquilly continued their work.'[24] The women who went to court could not understand why all of the women and girls involved in the incident were not prosecuted. For example, the girls who assisted Hodgkins over the stile were not summonsed.

Apart from Emma Wright there was no record of other witnesses being called for the women and so the Bench discussed the case while Mr Rawlinson, the clerk of the court, defined the several clauses of the Act under which the charge had been laid. One of the magistrates, Reverend Carter, asked Hambidge if he really wanted to press charges against the women, two of whom had babies with them. Mr Hambidge replied, 'It is very bad that I am not able to get anyone to work. What am I to do?'[25]

Reverend Carter agreed, but pointed out that Hambidge should realise that the trial itself would serve as a warning. He said he could not contemplate the thought of the women being sent to prison. Hambidge pressed his case, whereupon Reverend Carter replied that 'there was then no other alternative than to convict, the Act prescribing no fine'.[26] After further discussion, the Bench concluded that the case against the defendants had been clearly proved.

The magistrates, who were first and foremost Church of England vicars and not legally trained, did not seem to realise that one option was to let the women out on their own recognisance. Nor did they seem to be aware that the previous year, the presiding Justices had taken that option when some men were summonsed before the Woodstock Bench under the very same Act, even though some slight violence was proved. Since then, there had been no threatening or intimidation in the neighbourhood of Woodstock, and it had not been necessary to require the men to come up for judgement. It should also have occurred to the magistrates that the women may not have known they had committed any offence, being ignorant of the Criminal Law Amendment Act passed in 1871.[27]

The seven women who were considered the ringleaders were sentenced to ten days with hard labour. The charge sheet[28] listed:

Martha Smith, 45, married, born in Shilton, labourer, Church of England;
Mary Moss (otherwise Smith), 17, single, born in Ascott-under-Wychwood, servant, Baptist;
Charlotte Moss, 39, married, born in Ascott-under-Wychwood, labourer, Church of England;
Ann Susan Moss, 25, married, born in Chipping Norton, labourer, Church of England;
Fanny Honeyborn [sic], 16, single, born in Ascott-under-Wychwood, gloveress, Baptist;
Ann Moss, 22, married, born in Stanton Harcourt, labourer, Church of England;
Rebecca Smith, 25, married, born in Churchill, labourer, Church of England.

The remaining nine women, sentenced to seven days with hard labour, were:

Martha Moss, 33, married, born in Mixbury, gloveress, Church of England;
Caroline Moss, 18, single, born in Ascott-under-Wychwood, gloveress, Church of England;
Elizabeth Pratley, 29, married, born in Burford, labourer, Church of England;
Mary Pratley, 33, married, born in Hailey, labourer, Methodist;
Lavinia Dring, 44, born in Ascott-under-Wychwood, gloveress, Baptist;
Amelia Moss, 36, married, born in Ascott-under-Wychwood, gloveress, Baptist;
Jane Moss, 31, married, born in Ascott-under-Wychwood, gloveress, Baptist;
Ellen Pratley, 25, married, born in Leafield, gloveress, Baptist;
Mary Moss, 35, married, born in Ascott-under-Wychwood, gloveress, Baptist.

All sixteen women were recorded as living in Ascott-under-Wychwood in 1873.

Having been found guilty, the women were removed from the court; the husbands who were there were allowed to see their wives, as long as the men promised to leave town in an 'orderly manner'. The men left the Chipping Norton police station and returned to Ascott-under-Wychwood.

According to the *Oxfordshire Weekly News*, the women and babies were then 'thrust in two dark cells, eight in each. Owing to the confined spaces they sat on the pallet and stood by turns, the two babies wailing pitifully the whole time.'[29] The women tried to pacify their hungry, distressed babies and loosened their clothing. They would have heard the shouting of the milling crowd outside and been frightened about what lay ahead.

CHAPTER 6: THE RIOT
'PULL DOWN the POLICE STATION!'

After the trial, a local carrier, Richard Weaver, heading home to Ascott-under-Wychwood, met William Pratley on the Burford Road at about 6 p.m. William accepted a ride and sat on a barrel of beer on the cart.[1] They reached Ascott soon after 7 p.m. and told others what had happened. William's wife, Elizabeth, was not charged, but she could have been one of the women involved in picketing who was not summonsed. William may have gone to Chipping Norton to support his brothers' wives, Mary Pratley and the other Elizabeth Pratley.

William and some of the husbands, with other union men, returned to Chipping Norton that same evening and 'marched with blue ribbons floating from their hats to the police station' on Rock Hill.[2] They planned to rescue the women from the custody of the police as they were being taken to the railway station to catch the last train to Oxford, leaving at 7:40 p.m.[3]

Two other men had been convicted in another trial that day, which added to the excitement in the town. By about 7 p.m. a crowd had gathered in High Street near the police station to catch a glimpse of the convicted men and, supposedly, the women being taken to the railway station. Among the crowd were husbands and friends of the convicted women, who demanded their release, 'or else', they said to Superintendent Lakin, they would 'pull the police station down'.[4]

This signalled another outcry from the crowd, about 1,000 to 1,200 strong. They gathered closer around the police station, throwing more stones, which broke windows and roof tiles. A door was also broken. The glass in the street lamp standing nearby was completely shattered. The crowd shouted, 'Fetch the women!', 'Stick to the union!', 'Cheers for the women!'

and 'Cheers for the union!', along with further threats that they would pull the police station down unless the women were freed.[5]

Word soon got around the district, and the crowd grew even larger. Superintendent Lakin 'deemed it inadvisable to take the women through the town to the station'.[6] So shortly after 7 p.m., Thomas Norgrove, one of the two men convicted earlier in the day, was the only one taken to the railway station in the custody of a police constable. He had been found guilty of larceny at Milton and sentenced to several weeks' imprisonment.[7]

By 9 p.m. the open space in front of the police station was packed. Superintendent Lakin sent a telegram for assistance to Oxford, some 19 miles away. On receiving it, Inspector Yates gathered a force of police and started out in a drag and four, stopping at Woodstock to pick up Superintendent Bowen. The journey would take some four hours.

Meanwhile, back in Chipping Norton, the growing crowd continued their cries to free the women, and more threats were made to pull the station down. Interspersed with this were shouts in support of the union. Disparaging remarks were also made about the farmer, Robert Hambidge.[8] At about 10 p.m. the Mayor, Mr A. L. Rawlinson, with Aldermen J. Farwell and William Bliss, appeared on the scene and tried to persuade the crowd to disperse. Threats to read the Riot Act were in vain.

The 'most riotous in the crowd were a number of artisans from Heythrop, who are engaged on the new mansion now in the course of erection for Mr Brassey'.[9] Heythrop is a village on the outskirts of Chipping Norton. The mason, Edward Belcher of Chipping Norton, being somewhat drunk, threw stones and shouted, 'Stick to the union, who stole the donkey, fetch out the women.' He also sang union songs. A rather large stone shattered one of the window shutters of Superintendent Lakin's residence above the police station. Belcher was charged, fined 17 shillings and sentenced to 21 days hard labour.[10]

William Barry, another mason from Chipping Norton, threw a stone at a lamp in the passage leading to the guard room in the police station. He was taken to court and fined £2 12s 0d.[11] Charles Stroud, a mason from Over Norton, threw several stones at the street lamps, breaking them, which resulted him being fined £1 16s 0d.[12]

William Pratley must have returned to Chipping Norton quickly because he was amongst the crowd, and shouted, 'Hurrah for the union! Stick to the union you …'. Elizabeth's husband, Eli, was found with his brother William

'PULL DOWN the POLICE STATION!'

in the King's Arms in Chipping Norton and ordered home by a constable. William was subsequently charged with being drunk and disorderly in Town's End, Chipping Norton, and was fined, with costs, 17 shillings.[13]

Fanny and Jane Honeybone's brother-in-law, Thomas Rainbow, also part of the drunk and disorderly faction, tried to address the crowd, urging them to 'fetch the women out'. Thomas was charged with being drunk and disorderly on Rock Hill, but this was not proven and the case was dismissed.[14] Amelia's husband, George Moss, drunk, tried to force his way into the police station, shouting, 'We have come for our wives, and we will pull the... police station down... go to it boys, stick to the union!' He

The Chipping Norton Police Station showing the holding cells. Inset: Inside one of the two holding cells where eight of the women and the two babies were held for several hours.

also shouted insults at Alderman William Bliss while he was addressing the crowd. George's brother William Moss later said in court that he had been with George for some of the time and swore that he 'was not in beer. I did not see him do anything. I can't say he was sober'. George was ordered to pay £1 11s 0d in fines and costs.[15]

William Hewer, a shoemaker of Bledington, in a drunken state waved a stick about and shouted, 'Come on boys, stick to the union. Fetch out the women!' He was duly fined 21 shillings.[16] Other rioters were also taken to court. Thomas Townsend, a fishmonger of Chipping Norton, pleaded guilty to being drunk and disorderly on Rock Hill on 21 May, and was ordered to pay 11s 6d in fines and costs.[17] William Allen, a labourer from Chipping Norton, was also charged with being drunk and disorderly on nearby Rock Hill on the same day. Although he denied the charge, Allen was ordered to pay 12s 6d in fines and costs.[18]

Joseph Hodgkins, town crier of Chipping Norton, was charged with wilfully damaging a public gas lamp, the property of the Corporation of Chipping Norton on 21 May. The Bench considered the case clearly proved, and fined the defendant £1 16s 0d, including costs and damages.[19] George Simms, a tailor from Over Norton, was charged with wilfully damaging the windows of the police station on the same night, and ordered to pay £1 8s 0d in fines and costs.[20] James Nunney, a plasterer of Chipping Norton, was charged with committing wilful damage, but as one of the witnesses who had been summonsed was not present, the case was remanded until 19 June.[21]

Under the headline 'Astounded', *The Times* of Monday 26 May reported 'the "roughs" of the neighbourhood, in which there is a manufactory, assembled in considerable force', mentioned the damage to the police station, the call for more police, and the sending of the women to prison. It also noted that 'petitions to the Home Secretary are spoken of in the district'. The threatening attitude of the villagers instigated the return of the police from Oxford on Saturday, three days after the trial.[22]

Back in Chipping Norton, William Bliss, who built and owned the Bliss Tweed Mill near the railway station, replied to the article in *The Times* with a letter defending his workers: 'mine being the only manufactory in the town, I (without wishing to mix myself up in this unfortunate affair) feel bound to vindicate my workpeople from any reflection contained in that remark.'[23]

'PULL DOWN the POLICE STATION!'

The chairman of the Oxford district of the National Agricultural Labourers' Union, Christopher Holloway, wrote to the *Chronicle* expressing dismay at the result of the court case. 'The witnesses swore that some of the women had sticks in their hands, and said to the men that they would not be allowed to go to work. The women denied this altogether.' He criticised the fact that there was no attempt to prove that physical force was used. He added that the women were very respectable for agricultural workers' wives.[24]

Holloway claimed responsibility for restraining the crowd's anger, and said that if he had not been there, more violence would have occurred. 'The people,' he wrote, 'were astonished and bewildered at the sentence passed on such a number of poor women for what appeared to be no offence.' He claimed that the women themselves had no idea of the law they were convicted under. He finished by saying that he had never been more shocked than 'to see these 16 poor women dragged off for prison, and some of them with infants at their breasts'.[25]

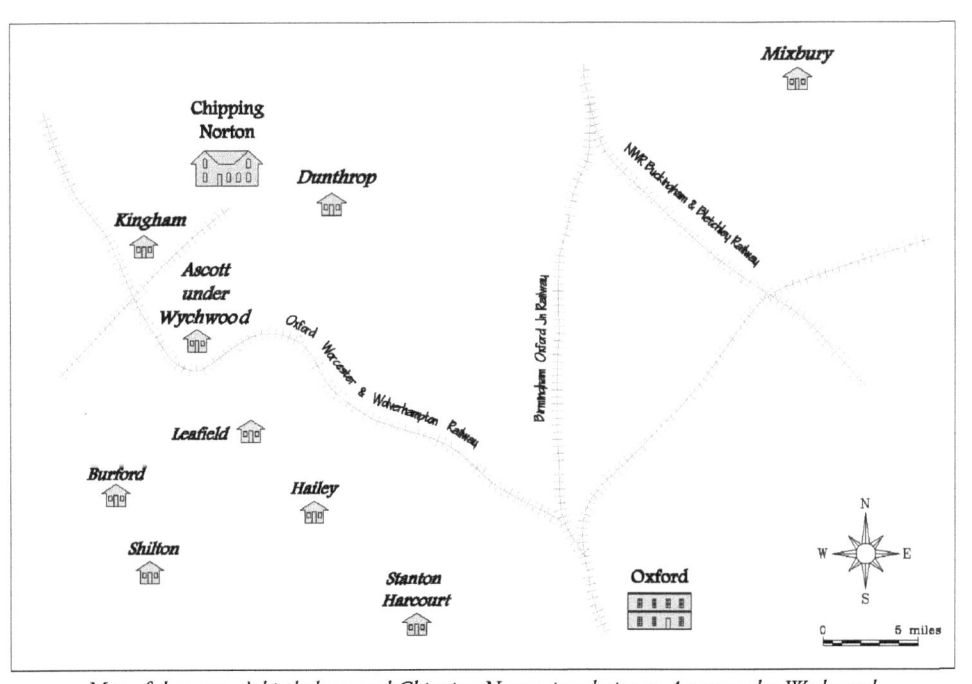

Map of the women's birthplaces and Chipping Norton in relation to Ascott-under-Wychwood.
(Charles Maaka, Auckland.)

CHAPTER 7: SENTENCED

PRISON with HARD LABOUR

By about midnight the crowd outside the police station in Chipping Norton had quietened down and started to depart. An hour later, when the drag arrived from Oxford with the extra policemen, accompanied by Inspectors Yates and Bowen, they had almost dispersed.[1] As soon as the police reinforcements arrived, the sixteen women and two babies were hurriedly bundled from their cells out into the cold air and onto the drag. Mary and Elizabeth Pratley did not have time to dress the babies, although they pleaded with Superintendent Lakin to let them do so. They wrapped the babies against the cold as best they could. It is not known whether the horses were replaced with fresh ones before the four-hour journey to Oxford County Gaol began.[2] The extra police stayed in Chipping Norton, although it remained peaceful.

The journey to Oxford was long and cold, and heavy dew fell. The women huddled together under their umbrellas to try to keep warm.[3] About half way, the group stopped at one of the Woodstock inns, and Inspector Yates bought the women bread and ale.[4] They arrived at the prison gate at 5 a.m.[5] In line with the general prison regulations of the time, the sixteen women were probably examined to check their health and cleanliness. They would have then bathed in cold or warm water, their clothes would have been taken away and fumigated,[6] and they would have been given prison clothes to wear.

They were probably in time for breakfast—a pint of oatmeal gruel. The seven women who had been convicted for ten days with hard labour received an additional six ounces of bread with the gruel. Dinner at midday was six ounces of bread each, and the evening meal was another pint of oatmeal gruel and six ounces of bread.[7] The gruel was to contain two ounces of oatmeal per pint, and on every other day was to be sweetened with three-quarters of an ounce of molasses or sugar, and seasoned with salt.[8] They were also given a pint of soup each during their stay, a weekly regulation. Each pint of soup was to contain three ounces of cooked meat without bone, three ounces of potatoes, an ounce of barley, rice or oatmeal, and an ounce of onions or leeks, with pepper and salt. In seasons when the potato crop failed, four ounces of split peas made into a pudding was substituted, but the change could not be made more than twice each week.[9]

Mary Pratley tried to continue breastfeeding her ten-week-old baby Thomas, but found it difficult. Although she did not have any trouble feeding him at home, in prison she did not have enough proper food to ensure an adequate milk supply. The bread and thin gruel was not enough. She needed cups of tea. Baby Thomas was used to having a little bread and milk with sugar, but the matron said that sugar was not allowed. Mary was permitted only half a pint of milk morning and evening to supplement Thomas's feeds. Neither the governor, the chaplain, the doctor, nor the visiting magistrates ever asked whether she had enough food for the child or herself, or whether she was breastfeeding the baby.[10] Baby Thomas developed a very bad cough, and by Sunday, Mary said he coughed until he was 'black in the face'.[11] Although the matron saw him, nothing was done.

Her sister-in-law Elizabeth also had only bread and gruel to eat. She was used to having milk, beer, meat, and broth at home. Her nine-month-old baby, Eli, received only three-quarters of a pint of milk twice a day, and none during the night. The matron gave a little of her daily sugar ration for his midday meal of bread and milk. At home little Eli always had plenty of sugar both with his milk and with his bread and milk mixture, as well as having milk to drink in the night. While in prison, he cried incessantly because he was hungry and cold in the damp cell.

His mother was also hungry and cold. The doctor came each morning and, on the first day, looked at her hands, but did not ask how she felt or how the baby was doing. Elizabeth hardly got an hour's sleep any night because her baby cried so much. The doctor saw her twice, but she said he never asked about the baby, or even looked at him. 'The child caught cold and coughed so much the night before last (Friday night) I thought it would have died.'[12]

Although Baby Eli was not unhealthy before he went into prison, he was never strong, and soon became a great deal worse. Elizabeth also got a very bad cold and developed rheumatism in her shoulders and limbs after the cold, wet night drive to Oxford. (A fuller version of Mary and Elizabeth Pratley's statements on prison conditions can be found in chapter 12.)

HARD LABOUR

For the duration of their imprisonment, fourteen of the women—Levia Dring; Jane, Martha, Caroline, Amelia, Mary, Charlotte, Ann Susan and Ann Moss; Martha and Rebecca Smith; Ellen Pratley, Fanny Honeybone and Mary Moss (otherwise Smith)—washed and ironed the prison laundry and mended prison clothes all day as part of their punishment.[13] Elizabeth and Mary Pratley were excused from the laundry work to look after their babies.[14]

An opinion of the time, no doubt that of a man, was that women committed to hard labour were actually considered fortunate as this entitled them to a more generous diet than that of women who were merely detained: 'to a healthy woman the labour is extremely light, owing to the number by whom it is shared'.[15] Writing to the Lord Chancellor, the Duke of Marlborough said that he thought the hard labour was scarcely a punishment, as he 'ascertained that it consists only of washing and ironing'.[16] Little did these men know of the effort needed to wash and iron clothes and bedding in a normal setting, let alone all day and every day in the prison laundry.

The laundry provided the chief source of income for the female prison, contributing more than half the money needed to support the prisoners. But the laundry was inadequate for the work required, with poor ventilation and overcrowding.[17] It was probably a room with a stone floor, 'complete with fires for heating the water, solid tubs, tables and various accessories such as a dolly—a wooden appliance with projecting prongs used to stir the washing and press it against the side of the tub'.[18] The wooden bat used to beat clothes to remove dirt and grime was called a 'beetle' or 'battledore'. The women would have 'beetled' away busily, as the saying went.[19]

The laundered articles were put through a mangle, involving boxes weighted with stones. These were moved backwards and forwards upon rollers to press sheets, tablecloths, and other flat linen spread upon the table beneath. Whether hand wringers—two rollers, initially of iron and later of wood, held with weighted levers or screws to allow the clothes to be passed between them[20]—had been installed by 1873 is not known.

Ironing involved smoothing out the wrinkles from freshly washed and dried clothes and linens. Originally, smooth stones were heated in the embers of a fire and then wrapped in a cloth to protect the hands, before pressing them over the fabric. In time, stones were replaced by flat irons, which again were heated on a grid above a fire and, later yet, upon a stove. To save time, a busy laundress would heat up several irons simultaneously, but in doing so risked them getting too hot and scorching the clothes or linens she was pressing.[21]

Washing, scrubbing, wringing, sorting, and folding hundreds of clothes, flannels and sheets 'was physically arduous and exhausting... involved a lot of sweat and toil and took up a great deal of time'. As well, there were probably articles from the prison infirmary, infested with 'all manner of diseases and other disgusting afflictions'.[22]

Women worked long hours standing at the tubs in the hot and steamy laundry. Each evening they returned to cold cells, their clothes wet from their day's work. If they were fortunate, the cell had a nail to hang up their wet things to dry overnight.[23] Each had a wooden bedstead and straw mattress with a rug and two blankets.[24] They also exercised in the yard for an hour each day.[25]

Above: Oxford County Gaol.
Insert: The main door of the Oxford County Gaol

CHAPTER 8: COPING AT HOME
THE WOMEN'S FAMILIES

While the women of Ascott-under-Wychwood were away in prison, their families had to manage without them and without their incomes. Altogether, 26 children had been left at home to be cared for.

Only six of the women (young Mary Moss, Fanny Honeybone, Ann Susan Moss, Ann Moss, Martha Moss, and Caroline Moss) did not have any children. Mary Moss's family included her mother Eliza, her stepfather Thomas (a carter and timber hauler), her sisters Emily (22, a gloveress) and Jane (3), and her brother Thomas (9). Fanny Honeybone's father, John, was an agricultural labourer on strike, and her mother, Jane, helped out at two farms just across the way from where they lived, or at the mill at the other end of the village. She also knitted socks, scarves, and shawls to sell.[1] Ann Susan Moss's husband, John, was also an agricultural labourer on strike, as was Ann Moss's husband, Caleb. Martha Moss's husband, William, was a sawyer. Caroline Moss's father, Joseph (69), was a carpenter and wheelwright. Her unmarried sister Harriet (28) was a gloveress, her brother Joshua (20) was an agricultural labourer on strike, and her niece Emily (7) lived with them.

Four of the married women—Ellen Pratley, and Amelia, Jane and Charlotte Moss—each had one child. Ellen Pratley's husband John, an agricultural labourer on strike, was left to care for their three-year-old son, John. Amelia Moss's husband, George, also an agricultural labourer on strike, was left with their daughter, three-year-old Julia. Jane Moss's husband, Robert, was a shepherd, and their son George was thirteen. Charlotte Moss's husband, William, was a railway servant, and their eleven-year-old son, William, went to school.

THE WOMEN'S FAMILIES

Two of the married women had three children each. Rebecca Smith and her husband Charles, an agricultural labourer on strike, had Sarah (7), George Allan (5), and Thomas (3). Elizabeth Pratley had nine-month-old Eli with her in prison, and her husband Eli, an agricultural labourer on strike, was left with their two young daughters, Elizabeth (4), and Ellen, aged two. The children's grandparents William and Maria Osman lived in Burford some six miles away and possibly took them in. The 1871 census records that Elizabeth Pratley and her daughter Elizabeth were staying with the Osmans about the time her second child, Ellen, was born. In later years, young Elizabeth lived in Burford with her grandparents until they died.

The other women had larger families. Levia Dring's husband, James, an agricultural labourer on strike, had four daughters to care for: Emma (16), Annie (15), Mary Jane (13), and Alice (11). Martha Smith had six daughters, but only three were living at home when she went to prison. Ellen Jane (15) was living and working in the household of farmer William Lardner. Eliza (14) was living and working in the household of Robert Hambidge. Rachel (11), Jane Maria (9), and Elizabeth Leah (6) were at school. Another daughter, Louisa, born in 1869, had died at eighteen months.

Mary Pratley, married to Frederick, an agricultural labourer on strike, had six children, five of whom (George (10), Frederick (8), John William (6), Charles Ernest (4), and three-year-old Mary Ann) needed to be cared for while she was in prison with baby Thomas.

Levia Dring, sisters-in-law Martha and Rebecca Smith, and Mary and Elizabeth Pratley all lived close to each other, so perhaps the older girls in these families looked after the younger children while their fathers worked several miles away each day to bring in some money.

The Ascott school report for Wednesday 21 May 1873 recorded:

Wednesday's attendance was bad, owing to the wet weather, and to the excitement caused by the summoning of nearly 20 [mothers] some married, some single by Mr Hambidge for attempting to prevent two Ramsden men from coming to work for him. The attendance towards the end of the week diminished through the parents of some of the absent children being included in the sixteen women of the village committed to prison.[2]

John Timms was seven in 1873. His mother was not charged, but fifty years later he could remember the time when the women were in prison. With his family, he had emigrated to New Zealand in 1874 on the same ship as Eli and Frederick Pratley and their families, Edwin and Harriet Smith and their family, and Peter Honeybone and his family, all from Ascott-under-Wychwood.

When John spoke to an audience who had gathered in 1925 for a reunion of the immigrants of the clipper ship *Crusader*, he told them that when the women went to prison, the Agricultural Union had made arrangements to feed the children, irrespective of whether their fathers were union members or not. According to John, the children had never had such a good time in their lives. For once their stomachs were full, for they were all given more than plenty to eat. He recalled that on the Sunday, a general invitation was sent out to all of the other children of the village to come and join in with the midday meal. On the table was a big bowl of soup, as well as joints of English roast beef and boiled legs of mutton, with cabbage, potatoes, and turnips. After they had finished all the meat and vegetables they could eat, one of the largest plum puddings he had ever seen appeared. 'And it was a plum pudding, with the emphasis on the plums! And although it did not contain the number of ingredients which the King's Christmas pudding was reported to have in it, nevertheless it was fit for any king.' John recalled that it was wonderful how quickly that pudding disappeared, and it was served in such liberal quantities that no one needed a second helping.[3]

So the union stepped in and fed the children. At first the food was brought in daily from a neighbouring village, and 'the deserted little ones, to the number of a score upwards, were fed on the village green, under the shade of the spreading chestnuts...'[4] Evidently it was suggested that eating outside was hardly appropriate, so the meals were then served in a small cottage opposite the village wheelwright's shop, supervised by an old woman who was reported to be 'only too pleased at having the opportunity of doing so'.[5]

CHAPTER 9: RELEASED
'THEY BE MARTYRS to a GOOD CAUSE'

On Wednesday 28 May 1873, seven days after they had entered the County of Oxford Gaol, nine of the sixteen women were released. Levia Dring; Amelia, Jane, Mary, Martha and Caroline Moss; Ellen Pratley, Elizabeth Pratley holding baby Eli, and Mary Pratley carrying baby Thomas, all clean and respectably dressed, walked out of the gaol at 10:20 a.m. The women acknowledged, with thanks, that they had received kindness from the officials at the prison, and that everything the prison regulations allowed was done for them.

They were greeted by a number of people who had gathered outside the gaol gates. A special delegation, including Christopher Holloway, chairman of the Oxford district branch of the union; Henry Taylor, the secretary of the union; and Josiah Godden of Woodstock, a member of the Consultative Committee of the National Agricultural Labourers' Union, were waiting to welcome them, along with two of the husbands.[1]

When the women appeared, a few disapproving persons cried, 'Shame!' But one man remarked, 'They be martyrs to a good cause',[2] and the majority of the crowd agreed. The women were taken directly from the prison to the nearby National Agricultural Labourers' Union office on Botley Road, where Joseph Leggett, the district secretary of the Oxford branch, lived. There they were given a 'liberal and substantial meat breakfast, tea, cake, bread and butter, ham etc'.[3]

About midday they left the union office and went back along Botley Road to the Great Western Railway station, where they caught the express to Chipping Norton junction. When the train passed through Ascott-under-Wychwood, 'the window of one carriage was blocked up with hands waving handkerchiefs, and a number of chubby children looking over the blossoming hedgerows in the village cried with delight on recognising their mothers'.[4]

The union paid for their train fares, and the time of departure was kept secret, in case a crowd gathered and caused another demonstration. Apart from the two husbands who met them at Oxford and travelled home with them, the other men were advised to stay away, so that there would be no risk of disruption leading to another riot.[5] Josiah Godden and Christopher Holloway, who also travelled with the women, went on to Leamington to take part in the General Conference of the union.[6]

The women waited an hour at the Chipping Norton junction before catching a train back to Ascott-under-Wychwood. The police chiefs, anticipating more trouble when the women returned home, sent telegrams to the various divisions in the county for police to go to Chipping Norton. Policemen came from Oxford, Banbury, Bicester, Deddington and other places, under the command of Captain Owen, the Chief Constable; Superintendent Cope, of Witney; Superintendent Lakin, and Inspector Jones.[7] Several plain clothes policemen were also present, so the authorities were fully prepared for any emergency. The activity of the extra police in and around the Chipping Norton railway station was somewhat disturbing, and there was an air of expectation that more trouble might occur.[8] As it happened, the police were not needed, and they had to put up with a considerable amount of jeering as they paraded through the town. However, a posse of police was also sent to Ascott-under-Wychwood, just in case of trouble there.[9]

When the women reached Ascott-under-Wychwood, their children and some friends were waiting to greet them. Reportedly there was much joy as the mothers were reunited with their children, other family members, and friends. Meanwhile, the inspector in charge of the posse appeared embarrassed to have such a force mustered against the tidy and well-behaved group. He fixed his gaze upon a rook's nest in the nearest tree until the group moved on out of sight. No threat or anger had surfaced in Ascott-under-Wychwood since the trial, and the husbands of the women regarded the extra police presence as insult added to injury.[10]

Once again the school reported that, 'the attendance on Wednesday afternoon was bad, caused by the return to the village of nine of the women from prison at Oxford and in the evening to be addressed by Mr Joseph Arch, Banbury,[11] and [Reverend] Attenborough ...'[12] (A description of the evening celebration is given in chapter 13.)

The Reverend Frederick Samuel Attenborough's support for the union contrasted markedly to the positions taken by the two Church of England vicars, the Reverends Harris and Carter, who, acting as magistrates, had sat in judgement on the women's case (see chapter 10). Born about 1842 in Erdington, Warwickshire, Attenborough attended Independent College, Withington, as a theological student in 1861. In 1866 he married Mary (maiden name unknown), who came from London, and by 1871 they had a three-year-old son, Frederick. In 1871 the Reverend Attenborough was a minister at the Congregational Church, Holly Walk, Leamington, Warwickshire. He was a 'notable' friend of the union,[13] and became treasurer of the Warwickshire Labourers' Union.[14] Sadly, his work with the union was short-lived. He died in 1879, aged 37, leaving Mary with four children: Frederick (11), Harold (6), John (2), and baby Gladys. In 1881 Mary, aged 37, was living with her children in Russell Terrace, Leamington, and was a newspaper proprietor. Son Frederick later became a journalist in Leicestershire; Harold, a chemist in Somerset; John, a journalist and author, and Gladys, a governess.

After the women arrived home, their friends said that some of the evidence given in court by Hambidge and the two youths was false, even though they had sworn under oath to tell the truth. The convicted women unanimously agreed, and friends wondered how the statements of two 'raw' youths could prevail over the testimony of sixteen respectable women. Answers were needed.[15]

EARLY PRESS REPORTS

The *Oxfordshire Weekly News* of 28 May 1873 reported the committal of the sixteen women, the riot, the trial of the rioters, the Home Secretary's inquiry into the conduct of the magistrates (presumably a result of the petitions mentioned in *The Times*), and the impending release of the nine women serving seven days. On 11 June 1873, the same paper again reported the committal of the sixteen women for intimidating the two would-be strike-breakers. It also published a copy of an article from the *Standard* criticising the action of the magistrates, along with reports on the release of the remaining seven women the previous Saturday, and the agricultural labourers' demonstration in Chipping Norton.

While the women were in prison, an article entitled 'Magistrates and Women at Chipping Norton' was written by Archibald Forbes, as the special correspondent for the *Daily News*. He thought that the successful growth of 'Mr Arch's movement into these purely agricultural districts would not have been so deep had not the wives of the labourers espoused the cause with unflagging earnestness'. In his opinion, the women believed the union would eventually succeed in getting the wage of twelve shillings increased to fourteen shillings a week.[16]

Forbes, who had recently accompanied a party of emigrants selected partly from Oxfordshire and partly from the Buckinghamshire district, noticed that the women were, in most instances, 'the ruling spirits. But for them the little allotment and the uneventful routine of the hamlet would never have been given up.'[17] It was the women who, when the ship started on its way, started singing the 'jubilant songs and choruses which gave life and cheerfulness to an otherwise dismal scene.' So he was not surprised to find this generally peaceful district in the throes of a small revolution because of the women's actions to improve the lot of their families.

THE QUEEN VICTORIA STORY

When the women were sent to prison, pleas for an early release had been made to the Home Secretary, but no response was received. Although the first group of nine women had by this time already been freed, it was not too late for an early release for the seven women still in prison.

Historian Ralph Mann stated in his unpublished notes[18] that Queen Victoria herself became involved, and ordered a Royal Pardon for the women. All that is definitely known, however, is that on 29 May 1873, at 1:39 p.m., a telegram was despatched from the Secretary of State to the Governor of the County Gaol, Oxford. It read:

> I have advised Her Majesty to remit that part of the sentence of the women still in custody under committal by the Chadlington bench of magistrates which imposed hard labour in addition to imprisonment they are not therefore to be kept any longer at hard labour and official authority will follow in due course.[19]

On Saturday 31 May, the Governor of Oxford Gaol received the Queen's Warrant to remit the remainder of the women's sentences and to release them forthwith; but as the whole sentence expired that same day, the warrant had no practical effect.

There was also a widely circulated story that after the women had all been discharged, Queen Victoria gave each of them a red flannel petticoat and five shillings, yet there is no mention of this in her diaries. Any interest in the women's imprisonment would have been overtaken by the death of her little grandson at Balmoral Castle on Thursday 29 May 1873,[20] the day after the first nine women were released. No newspaper report of the petticoat story can be found either. If this did happen, it is possible that the petticoats and money were delivered to the prison for one of the wardens to distribute. Jane, Dowager Lady Churchill, from nearby Blenheim Palace in Woodstock, may also have been involved, as she was a Lady in Waiting to the Queen.

THE SECOND RELEASE

The remaining seven women, who had all served ten days of imprisonment with hard labour, were released from the County of Oxford Gaol at about 10 a.m. on Saturday 31 May: Ann Moss, Charlotte Moss, Ann Susan Moss, Martha Smith and Rebecca Smith, and the two youngest women, Fanny Honeybone and young Mary Moss.[21]

This was a much-celebrated occasion, with about 150 supporters, both men and women, waiting outside the prison gate. Mr Christopher Holloway, the president of the Oxford branch of the union; Mr Leggett, the secretary; and Mr Taylor, the general secretary of the union, were there, together with many 'sympathising friends'.[22] All accompanied the women to the union office in Botley Road and gave them a substantial breakfast of tea, coffee, bread, butter, ham and eggs, much enjoyed after a week of gruel and bread.[23]

Shortly before midday, the nine women left Oxford for Ascott-under-Wychwood, riding in a brake with four horses provided by a Mr Porter. Another crowd had gathered in front of the union office, and cheered loudly as the women set off. On their way via Woodstock and Chipping Norton, they passed through several villages and were cheered by villagers as 'martyrs to their cause'. As reported, the women looked very pleased with themselves.[24]

The party rested at Woodstock, where they were taken to dinner and treated very well. It was almost impossible for the women to move about, because so many people wanted to shake their hands and congratulate them. During this stop-over, Mr Holloway took the party into Blenheim Park, the seat of the Duke of Marlborough, whose antagonism to the union was well known. On leaving Woodstock there was loud cheering for the union, for President Arch, and for the women.

About 4 p.m., the four horses pulling the brake galloped across the Chipping Norton marketplace, with the driver blasting his horn to herald the women's arrival. This, together with an open-air meeting in their honour, had been advertised several days earlier, and many people had gathered for the occasion. On alighting, the women were led across the square to the King's Arms Inn where they were welcomed back with open arms by their husbands and relatives.[25]

The crowd included union sympathisers wearing the well-known slip of blue ribbon, as well as a number of the town tradespeople. By the time the public meeting was held in the square after tea, at 7 p.m., some 2,000 to 3,000 people had gathered: mainly male agricultural labourers, some with their wives, from all the surrounding districts. Ascott-under-Wychwood was well represented.[26] Union leaders Joseph Arch, Henry Taylor, Christopher Holloway, and Gabriel Banbury, along with Thomas Mottershead (representing the Reform Club of London) and others climbed onto a wagon drawn up in the square, and made the most of the opportunity to espouse the benefits of the union.[27]

Christopher Holloway opened the meeting by asking the crowd not to obstruct the roads and to let people and vehicles pass through. After all, they did not want any more arrests for obstruction. The women and the crowd clapped in approval. Mr Holloway said that not only was the union going to raise the wages of the agricultural labourers, but changes to some laws were also needed: three in particular. First, if the labourers' position was to improve, the franchise must be extended to households and to individual men, so that they could be eligible to vote and represent the needs of the labourers in Parliament. Second, the Criminal Law Amendment Act must be repealed, so that picketing could become legal. Third, a stipendiary magistracy was needed, so that paid magistrates could make fair judgements to all classes in law.

Gabriel Banbury stood and moved a resolution, seconded by Henry Taylor:
> That a clerical magistracy is most unsatisfactory, and in order to secure a better administration of the law this meeting considers it absolutely necessary to establish a stipendiary magistracy on account of the class interests brought to bear on the present administrators.[28]

Banbury's speech included praise for the women and the contribution they had made:
> They have given the Union which I have advocated an impetus that it had never received before. It has done a world of good to that Union and has been the means of bringing more men to it, and showing them what can be done by such a combination.[29]

Joseph Arch spoke at length in support of the resolution, which was put to the meeting and carried unanimously. Mottershead then proposed a second resolution:
> That the Criminal Law Amendment Act is, in its operation, unjust and oppressive towards the labouring classes of this country; this meeting therefore calls for its immediate and entire repeal.

It was seconded by G. F. Savage of Birmingham and enthusiastically carried.[30]

A resolution calling for the franchise to be extended to households was not put forward. Joseph Arch and Christopher Holloway were cheered and after a collection had been made on behalf of the women, the meeting broke up and the crowd dispersed.[31]

At last the women could go home to Ascott-under-Wychwood. Just another five miles, and they too would be reunited with their families.

CHAPTER 10: LEGAL REFORM

THE MAGISTRATES CRITICISED

The women's imprisonment gave rise to a great deal of comment and criticism relating to the two magistrates, Reverend Thomas Harris, BD, and Reverend William Edward Dickson Carter, MA, and their decision to sentence the women to prison with hard labour; the whole system of using clerical magistrates was also criticised.

Both magistrates lived amongst villagers similar to the women they sent to prison. At the time of the women's trial, they were living quite close to Ascott. Harris was about ten miles away to the north in Swerford, while Carter was only about three miles away in Sarsden.

The Reverend Thomas Harris, the older of the two, had grown up in Warwickshire, where the union had its first beginnings. Born in 1812 in Rugby, by 1851, aged 39, he was Rector of Swerford, living at the rectory with a housekeeper, a housemaid, and a gardener. Swerford is a village on the River Swere, in the Cotswold Hills in Oxfordshire, about four miles northeast of Chipping Norton. Ann Susan Moss's father was born in Swerford, and Ann Susan, in the nearby hamlet of Dunthrop.

Eight miles west of Swerford was the parish of Chastleton.[1] Next to the church was Chastleton House, a large Jacobean country house built between 1607 and 1612 by Walter Jones, a successful wool merchant and at one time MP for Worcester. Living in the house was John Whitmore Jones, magistrate for the County of Oxford, and his wife, Dorothy. They had several daughters, including Joanna Dorothea, who had been working as a governess and school mistress at a girls' school in Wanstead, Birmingham. Thomas Harris married Joanna some time between July and September 1851. He and his wife had no children; they continued to live in the rectory for the next twenty years.

THE MAGISTRATES CRITICISED

In 1873 Harris was still in Swerford and a magistrate for Oxfordshire. Aged 79 at the time of the trial, he was still the rector, and also a Justice of the Peace, living with Joanna and their three servants—a groom who was also the gardener, a cook, and a parlour maid. His connection with the Chastleton House family was probably very important to him, and it is likely that he would have wanted them to see him take a proper course with what would have been regarded as an unruly group of women. After all, the case against them was proven.

Reverend William Edward Dickson Carter was born in 1821 in Titchfield, a village in southern Hampshire, by the River Meon. His education included study at New College, Oxford University. In the first quarter of 1850, he married Ellen Barter. Ellen was born about 1831 in Sarsden, a hamlet in the parish of Churchill, Oxfordshire, where her father, Charles, was rector. She was one of ten children living in the Sarsden rectory in 1841, where the family was looked after by ten servants. Churchill, the nearby village, is situated in the triangle of Chipping Norton, Stow on the Wold and Burford. One of the sixteen Ascott women, Rebecca Smith, was born in nearby Kingham, and baptised in Churchill.

By 1871 Ellen Carter's father had died. She returned to the Sarsden rectory where she had grown up, with her husband and their six daughters: Ellen (20), who was born in Slapton,[2] Gertrude (14), Agatha (12), Agnes (11), Edith (9), and three-year-old Augusta, who were all born in Shipton-under-Wychwood. Their eldest son, William Collingwood Carter (18), was lodging with his cousin, George Markham, in Ryde, Hampshire, in a hotel kept by John Wavell, a pharmaceutical chemist. Also living with the family were a governess, laundry maid, cook, lady's maid, nurse, housemaid, under-housemaid, and groom.

The Reverend Carter also had connections, in his case with the tenant farmers and aristocracy, that might have influenced him to eventually agree with Reverend Harris's decision to imprison the women. In the parish of Churchill, and probably well known to the rectory family, stood Sarsden House, the home of James Haughton Langston MP, who was educated at Eton College and Christ Church, Oxford. A British landowner, he had inherited the Sarsden estate in 1812 after his father died. He was appointed High Sheriff of Oxfordshire for 1819–20, and verderer of Wychwood Forest, a place with which most of the women were familiar. He served as

MP for New Woodstock, near the Duke of Marlborough's Blenheim Palace, 1820–26, and then as MP for Oxford, 1826–34 and 1841–63.

James Langston married the Honourable Julia Moreton, daughter of Thomas Reynolds Moreton, first Earl of Ducie. Their only child, Julia, married her cousin, Lord Moreton, who later became the third Earl of Ducie. They lived at Tortworth Court, a Victorian mansion, in the parish of Tortworth near South Gloucestershire. In 1852 Lord Moreton entered Parliament as MP for Stroud. The following year he succeeded his father as earl and entered the House of Lords. In 1859 he was admitted to the Privy Council and appointed Captain of the Yeomen of the Guard under Lord Palmerston, a post he held until the government fell in 1866, the last year under the premiership of Lord Russell. In 1913 he became Father of the House of Lords, as its longest-serving member. Apart from his political career, Lord Ducie was Lord Lieutenant of Gloucestershire between 1857 and 1911, and Lord Warden of the Stannaries between 1888 and 1908.

Matthew Savidge farmed the 547 acres of Earl Ducie's estate, employing seventeen men and four boys. According to a diary kept by John Calvertt from Fairspear Farm in Leafield, near Ascott, Savidge knew the farmers of the Ascott area. The diary gives a good idea of the interconnections between the farmers and the aristocracy. This extract, written in 1875, shows that the farmers met with and were close to the political power wielders:[3]

> April 2. 1875... Drove to Mr Savidge's and accompanied him to Mr George Garne's, Churchill Heath, and witnessed a short-horned sale of 47 head—averaged £44.12s.0d. Earl Fitzhardinge was Chairman, supported by Lord Moreton (Earl Ducie's eldest son).... Tea'd at Mr Savidge's—John Charles (his son) accompanied me.[4]

Sarsden House was an easy ride of about three miles from Ascott-under-Wychwood. Farmers would meet each other at events such as cattle sales, sheep markets, horse fairs, and fox hunts. John Calvertt's diary records:

> April 9. Too wet for Thrashing, or Drilling. Met Hounds at Tangley, ran a fox 20 m. and killed him—tried Barrington Park covers blank, but found Biscuits, Bread & Cheese, Sherry, & Ale at the House—I came away for Shipton Sheep Auction... mutton 8 pence per lb. out of wool—Hounds went to Rissington, blank, and found at Gawcombe... Hounds ran away from all the 'Field' & killed in 45 m.: making 122 Foxes killed in 121 days Hunting: which excels any previous Heythrop Season!!! Tea'd at Mr. Maddox, and met Mr. Abraham after his tour with Spurgeon, to France, & Italy.[5]

Although in the end the Reverend Carter agreed with the Reverend Harris's decision, he was reported as shifting uneasily in his seat during the magisterial investigation. He was clearly aware that the sixteen women, two with babies, were placed in a most distressing position.[6] More than once he appealed directly to Mr Hambidge, asking him whether he wished to press the case. The Reverend Carter pointed out that the law permitted no fine to be levied, thus putting the magistrates in the painful position of sentencing the women to prison, unless Hambidge dropped the charges. Mr Hambidge remarked that dropping the case would cause great difficulty in getting men to come and work for him. As mentioned (see chapter 5) the Reverend Carter replied that the trial itself would be a warning to others, and would thus have the effect that Mr Hambidge desired; he feelingly remarked that he could not entertain the thought of the women being sent to Oxford Gaol.[7]

CHAPTER 11: SENTENCE UNDER SCRUTINY
CHANGE on the HORIZON

The Reverend Carter was right: the magistrates did not have the option of imposing a fine. However, they did have the option of binding the women over to keep the peace, instead of sending them to prison. This course had been followed in other incidents involving agricultural strike actions, with no further punishment necessary.[1] For example, as noted earlier, a similar case occurred in Woodstock in August 1872, when the Act forbidding picketing was breached to a greater extent. The men who went to court were found guilty of intimidating the victims as well as pushing them about. They were convicted and bound over to appear for judgement when called on. There was no more trouble from them, and they were never called. So while the Act did actually allow the penalty of imprisonment with or without hard labour for a term not exceeding three months, the magistrates were empowered to dismiss the offenders on their own recognisances. Yet Harris and Carter appeared not to know that this alternative was possible.

THE HOUSE of COMMONS

Soon enough, questions about the sentence were raised in the House of the Commons. On Monday 26 May, just four days after the women entered prison, the Home Secretary, Mr Bruce, was asked by Mr Mundella, Liberal MP for Sheffield and a reformer, whether it was true that sixteen women had been sentenced to imprisonment with hard labour by the Reverend Thomas Harris and the Reverend W. E. D. Carter at Chipping Norton, under the provision of the Criminal Law Amendment Act, and whether there was some justification to intervene and have the women released. The

Home Secretary replied that he had not received any communication on the subject, but he had directed that a letter be written to the magistrates that day. He received a reply three days later, Thursday 29 May, which he subsequently reported to the House.

Concern over the severity of the women's sentences highlighted the wider issue of unpaid, untrained clerical magistrates. Mr Auberon Herbert, MP for Nottingham, gave notice of his intention to move in the House of Commons that a request be made to the Queen to appoint a Royal Commission to look into all matters relating to the duties and appointment of magistrates. He did not deny that the women had threatened and intimidated two labourers from another village, 'in such a manner as would justify a Justice of the Peace, on complaint made to him, in binding over the person so threatening or intimidating to keep the peace'. The women had committed 'one of the very offences specified by the Criminal Law Amendment Act, and no honest jury could have acquitted them, however strongly it might have recommended them to mercy. It was not the conviction that was in question but the excessive sentence.'[2]

THE PRESS

Daily News correspondent Archibald Forbes roundly criticised the system of unpaid clerical magistrates who interpreted

> the severe provisions of a harsh Act with the most scrupulously unintelligent inattention to its terms, and carefully declining to take a lenient advantage of the looseness of its words, or to accept the option of a nominal penalty on a first, or a slight offence. Can we wonder if even the stolid and tranquil population of Chipping Norton was roused to indignation at the sight of these poor women, some of them with infants at their breast, being conveyed to prison upon such a charge, and such a sentence?
>
> The riot that followed is of course disgraceful to the village, but what shall be said of 'the great image of authority', as it presented itself last Wednesday on the Chipping Norton Bench, in the persons of two bewildered clergymen?
>
> There is something patriarchal in the power, office, and duty of these worthy gentlemen, who, as Blackstone[3] says, 'without any sinister views of their own, engage in this troublesome service'; and great lenity is shown by the superior Courts of Law to the occasional errors into which they may be betrayed by a rash or incompetent clerk, or by their over-confident and compendious ignorance of law.

He noted with sarcasm:

> A squire who gives up a day's shooting for the sake of his country while he sits on the bench and sentences a poacher is a splendid example of public spirit and patriotic self-denial; but a clergyman who takes his place beside the squire or with brother parson, and sits in judgment [sic] upon a labourer who has struck for higher wages, or a labourer's wife who has indulged in strong language and vehement gestures on behalf of 'Union principles', is evidently a far sublimer example.[4]

Continuing the irony, Forbes wrote that the National Agricultural Labourers' Union campaign for the repeal of the Criminal Law Amendment Act was 'indebted to the two Reverend Justices who presided on the magisterial bench of the day of the conviction and sentence'.[5] He also suggested that the women might 'console themselves with the reflection that the magistrates have made them martyrs'.

F. Clifford in *The Times* questioned why an appeal against the sentence had not been lodged by Christopher Holloway, or any other representative of the National Agricultural Labourers' Union, under the provisions of the Criminal Law Amendment Act. That Act expressly gave the right of appealing to Quarter Sessions to any person who felt 'aggrieved by any order or conviction made by a Court of summary jurisdiction'; if the appellant was in custody, the Justice had the discretion to release him.[6]

Perhaps, Clifford suggested, the Reverends Harris and Carter were not aware that they could let out the women on their own recognisance; but, he noted, it might have occurred to them that the women had committed the offence without knowing anything about the Criminal Law Amendment Act. Even so, he thought the two justices must have known that they could have omitted the hard labour. Union representative Christopher Holloway, in the courtroom waiting to pay a fine on behalf of the women, was possibly unaware that the justices had no power to inflict a fine. However, Forbes wrote, Holloway could have made an appeal to release them. This option too seemed to be overlooked.

Gabriel Banbury, the Oxford district treasurer, thought that some of the blame for the magistrates' decision lay with their legal advisor, the magistrates' clerk, who had the Act in front of him, and should have pointed out the discretionary power if the vicars were not aware of it. He also said that the bench was not the right place for clergy:

The pulpit was their place and in the houses of their flock, amongst the sick and poor, when they were copying the example of their great Master; but... in sitting in judgment [sic] they were not doing their Master's work.[7]

Banbury wondered if it were possible that the magistrates could not see they had other options than to send the women to prison. Like other supporters of the women, he made the point that they 'were not aware that they had violated the law'.[8]

After the women's imprisonment, the National Agricultural Labourers' Union worked towards the repeal of the Criminal Law Amendment Act, and the replacement of clerical magistrates with paid stipendiary magistrates, so that justice would be properly meted out to the labouring class.

THE LORD CHANCELLOR TAKES an INTEREST

The harshness of the sentence also roused the concern of the Lord Chancellor, Lord Selborne. On 4 June he wrote from 30 Portland Place to the Duke of Marlborough, who was the Lord Lieutenant. Selborne noted that Mr Bruce, the Home Secretary, had written to him about the two Justices of the Peace for the County of Oxford, on the subject of the recent conviction of sixteen women.

The Lord Chancellor had no doubt that the magistrates had sufficient proof of the offence, and he was also satisfied that the offence was a right and proper one for the magistrates to deal with seriously, being the result of an 'unlawful combination' against the freedom of labour, which, if not checked, might have spread'.[9] He informed the Duke that the convicting magistrates had told the Home Secretary that the sentence was the one that was required and 'they have since seen no reason for altering the opinion then formed'.

In Selborne's view, the real ends of justice were not served by sending so large a number of persons at the same time to prison in such cases. The magistrates had stated that the seven women sentenced to ten days' imprisonment with hard labour appeared to be the ringleaders; yet nine others were sentenced to seven days' imprisonment, also with hard labour. Even if it were proper to punish the seven women considered to be ringleaders, he thought that it was not necessary to impose a punishment so nearly the same, or actually any punishment at all, on the nine whose offence was not as serious.

While noting that unlawful combination involved danger to society and thus required repression by law, Selborne said that those gathering together were not necessarily lawbreakers, but were influenced by others to take part in such actions, sometimes against their will. This should 'weigh greatly' against the infliction of severe and indiscriminate penalties against large numbers of people. He believed that the use of such penalties would create sympathy with the lawbreakers, thus countering any practical benefit of the law.

The Lord Chancellor also said that the sex, ages, and condition of the offenders should have been taken into account, although he did note that the Reverend Carter tried to dissuade Mr Hambidge from pressing the case, urging him to consider the distress and pain imprisonment would cause the women and the two babies. But Carter appeared to have finally concurred with Harris in sentencing the women to prison with hard labour. He, Selborne, did not agree with that sentence, and asked the Duke to pass the letter on to the Reverends Harris and Carter; he would be pleased to hear their view, and also the Duke's, on the subject.[10]

The Duke of Marlborough, as previously noted, was antagonistic towards the unions. Nevertheless he summoned the two magistrates to explain their actions. He then wrote to the Lord Chancellor enclosing their replies. The Duke agreed with the Lord Chancellor that while the sentence was kept within the law, his own view was that the magistrates had chosen 'to exercise their own discretion in that Sentence, guided by the merits and the surrounding circumstances of the case, and that in this instance such discretion was exercised unwisely'.[11]

The issue of clerical magistrates was addressed in the House of Commons on Friday 6 June. Mr Downing MP asked Mr Gladstone, Prime Minister and First Lord of the Treasury, if he was aware that in Ireland a rule had been in force for many years in which clergymen of all denominations 'have been excluded from the Commission of the Peace in that country, and whether he was prepared to apply the same rule to other portions of the United Kingdom'.[12]

Mr Gladstone replied that the case was not exactly parallel to that in Ireland, and that he needed time to establish the facts before any decision was made:

> I have requested the Home Secretary to obtain some return information showing not only the actual number of clerical magistrates in this country, but also the course of

practice in late years, which undoubtedly has tended to a very great extent—and I think it a salutary tendency—to restrict materially the number of such magistrates.[13]

SUPPORT for the MAGISTRATES

Support for the magistrates and their actions came, predictably, from the landowners and tenant farmers. An anonymous communication from London, signed 'A Lover of Order', was received by the churchwardens of Ascott-under-Wychwood on 3 June. It claimed that the magistrates had:

> only done their duty—a very painful one no doubt, but that they were quite right in doing it is the opinion of all those who wish for any order. The ridiculous hue and cry that the radical 'Times' paper has got up is merely to serve a political purpose, and I hope that these gentlemen will stand against what is a most shameful attack on the laws of the country. I am sure they will not want for supporters. The object is that the labouring classes should govern the country, and in this case the men thought to evade the law by putting the women in their place ...[14]

Another correspondent signed himself 'Chipping Norton landlord':

> It is refreshing to turn from the comments of the London liberal press on the Chipping Norton rebellion to your sensible and appropriate remarks—that the law was broken—justice administered—the farmer protected—the farm labourer rebuked.... The sympathy of the Liberal Press is with the Ascott women who unsexed themselves, the mob who broke the peace and the committee of the Labourers' Union who are fanning the embers of agricultural discontent into an open blaze from John O'Groats to Land's End.[15]

At the opening of the Chadlington Petty Sessions on Wednesday 18 June, a large deputation of 'principal inhabitants' (that is, tenant farmers and landlords) from 31 villages, including Ascott, Sarsden, and Swerford, addressed Reverend Harris and Reverend Carter. They expressed their approval 'of the course then adopted by you, and hope that the sentence passed upon the offenders will check any further attempts to interfere with the freedom of labour. And we also beg to tender our thanks for your able and impartial administration of justice on the Bench for so many years past.'[16] The Reverends Harris and Carter replied with their 'profuse heartfelt thanks'. The deputation handed the address to the magistrates, then withdrew. Another similar address, signed by ten men, was presented by a deputation from Leafield.[17]

As later chapters show, the matter did not end there. The Ascott martyrs undoubtedly influenced and probably hastened judicial reform.

CHAPTER 12: MOTHERING IN PRISON

THE TREATMENT of the WOMEN and THEIR BABIES

How the two sisters-in-law with babies, Elizabeth and Mary Pratley, were treated in prison, was of great concern to barrister, and union supporter, Mr William Mackenzie of Trevor Square, Knightsbridge. He visited the two women in their homes on Sunday 1 June, four days after their release. In a letter to *The Times* he wrote:

> I took down the statements of the two women from their own lips in their own cottages yesterday morning. The women, though very poor, and living in miserable habitations, had every appearance of being respectable and trustworthy persons.[1]

Mary Pratley's statement read:

> I was nursing my baby from the breast, the child was only ten weeks old; I had as good a breast of milk as any woman in England when I went into prison, but while there had scarcely any, owing to my not having proper food. I had nothing but bread and skilly; I felt the want of tea very much. I got rheumatism in my shoulders and limbs very bad, chiefly I think, owing to the night drive [from Chipping Norton to the prison], which was both cold and wet. The doctor came each morning; he looked at my hands the first day. He made no enquiry about my state or that of the baby. My baby was taken away undressed from Chipping Norton police station in the middle of the night. I begged Superintendent Lakin to give me time to put the child's clothes on, but he refused, saying, 'you must come at once, there is no time to mess about.' We were placed in the open van. I wrapped up the child the best way I could in its clothes. The child took a very bad cough, and coughed until it was black in the face on the Sunday when we were in prison, and the matron saw it. My baby was accustomed to have a little sop with sugar. I told the matron that the child would not take the sop without sugar. She said no sugar was allowed. I was allowed only half a pint of milk morning and evening for the child. Neither the governor, nor the chaplain, nor the doctor, nor the visiting magistrates ever

asked whether I had food enough for the child or myself, or whether I was suckling the baby. (Mary Pratley +her mark. June 1)[2]

Elizabeth Pratley's read:

I had nothing while in prison but bread and skilly, no milk, beer, or meat or broth. My baby, seven months old, was with me.[3] I received for it what they called a pint, but it was not more than three-quarters of a pint of milk, twice a day, not near enough for the child. No milk was allowed for the child during the night time; only a very little sugar once a day for the child's sop at dinner time. At home it always had plenty of sugar both with its milk and its sop, and always some milk in the night. The child suffered very much from want of proper nourishment and from there being no fire in the cell. I also suffered from want of better food and from cold. I could hardly sleep at nights. I hardly got an hour's sleep any night. The child could not sleep at night it was so hungry. The doctor saw me twice but made no inquiry about the baby, nor ever looked at it. The child caught cold and coughed so much the night before last (Friday night) I thought it would have died. The child was not unhealthy, but was never strong, and has been a great deal worse since. I got a very bad cold from travelling by night, and from the dampness of the prison cell, I could hardly speak the day after I came home, my throat and chest were so bad and my limbs ached so. I am still not well by a long way. (Elizabeth Pratley +her mark. June 1)[4]

Mr Mackenzie thought that it was up to the Home Secretary, Mr Bruce, to institute an inquiry into the truth of the charge of gross inhumanity perpetuated by the authorities of the prison upon the two mothers and their infants, one ten weeks and the other seven months old.

On 4 June, a covering letter, enclosing Mackenzie's letter to *The Times* and the two statements by the women, was sent by the Home Secretary to the visiting justices of Oxford Castle, requesting a report about the treatment of Mary and Elizabeth Pratley and their babies while they were in prison. Two days later, Mr Edgar Alfred Bowring, Liberal MP for Exeter (1868–74), asked the Home Secretary if he could inform the House of the result of the inquiries he had made with reference to the Chipping Norton case; and whether there was any truth in the statements that the infants of two of the imprisoned women were insufficiently supplied with food during the period of their mothers' incarceration.[5] The Home Secretary replied that he had not heard or received anything from the prisoners themselves or from anybody else on their behalf. He had seen a statement on the subject in the papers, and 'desired inquiry to be made of the visiting justices as to its accuracy, but no answer has been received.'[6]

The following Saturday, 7 June, at 11:30 a.m., a meeting was held with the visiting justices at the Oxford prison to inquire into the treatment of the two women and their babies. In her report on Elizabeth Pratley, dated 7 June 1873, the matron said that the prisoner received a full measured pint of new milk for her baby, half a pint in the morning and half a pint in the evening, and six ounces of bread. The matron also said the baby was about seven months old, and in addition to the above diet she made it some sop with sugar, giving up her own sugar for it because the prisoner told her that the child had been used to having sugar. The matron asked the prisoner each day whether the child had everything it required for the night and she always got a satisfactory and contented answer. There does not seem to have been any report by the prison matron on the treatment of Mary Pratley and her baby.

The gaoler reported that Elizabeth Pratley was placed in an ordinary cell. None of the prison cells had a fire. The temperature of the cell was, according to the thermometer, from 55 degrees to 60 degrees Fahrenheit (between 12 and 15 degrees Celsius) throughout her imprisonment. It was a certified cell on the third floor, which was never damp but perfectly dry. The prisoner made no complaint to the gaoler at all. The matron said that the women never complained about the cold or dampness, although one complained of rheumatism; she was asked if she would like to see the doctor, but she refused. The matron had not noticed that one child (ten-week-old Thomas Pratley, Mary's son) had a cough.

In the House of Commons on Monday 9 June, the Home Secretary, Mr Bruce, said he had received a reply from the visiting justices of Oxford with respect to the treatment of the two women and children during their imprisonment. Complaints had been made as to the insufficiency and the quality of the food, general neglect, and also the absence of inquiry by the prison authorities or the visiting justices as to their treatment.

The Chairman of Quarter Sessions had reported that the visiting justices went to the prison on 24 May; that they saw all the women and asked them if they had any complaint to make; the women answered that they had no complaint. Two surgeons also said that the women were healthy and received sufficient food, and that when asked if they had any complaint to make, they made none. Mr Bruce reported the matron's statement to the House, though he did not point out that she had not mentioned Mary Pratley and her very young baby at all.

THE TREATMENT of the WOMEN and THEIR BABIES

Who was to be believed? The matron, or Mary and Elizabeth Pratley? William Mackenzie once again responded to the *The Times* report of this session in the House. He said that he had never suggested that the treatment of the women in gaol was not in agreement with the prison rules; but he disagreed, because a nursing mother should have more than the bread and gruel offered. He also noted that when the two women were asked if there were any complaints, in front of the governor, the matron, and two justices, they would feel it was useless to complain, because they knew they would be told 'they were treated in accordance with the regular practice in such cases'. Mackenzie ended his letter thus:

> it is of this regular practice that I venture to complain; and if what has now transpired should lead to an alteration in the scale of diet allowed to women nursing children, while under the confinement of prison, many hapless mothers and innocent babes will have reason to be grateful...[7]

After the women were released, reporter Archibald Forbes met with Alfred Moss, a journeyman wheelwright and husband to the older Mary Moss, and arranged an interview later that same afternoon with some of the other released women in Mary and Alfred's house.[8] His report suggested that the British public would be somewhat amazed if they could have seen the description of the women who had been receiving 'felons' treatment for an action in which they declared they had no malicious motive, and which was accompanied by no single threat or act of intimidation.'[9]

Their home was, he wrote, in sharp contrast to the old workhouse where Elizabeth and Mary Pratley lived (see chapter 1). There were pictures on the wall and ornaments on the mantelpiece. A coconut mat covered the floor. A sideboard was well stocked with plates and dishes. The flesh of a couple of pigs hung under the ceiling, where they were smoked from the rack above the fireplace. Three of Mary's friends, all gloveresses, were in the house when Mr Forbes visited. They were probably Levia Dring and cousins Martha and Caroline Moss. He said all were well dressed and well spoken; in fact, they were typical of lower middle-class Englishwomen. A white tablecloth was spread and there were two joints of meat on the table ready for tea. The reporter was a little uncomfortable at intruding. Mary smiled and offered to help him 'all she could...'[10]

The women told Forbes their version of what happened and said that after the sentence was pronounced in court, they believed their husbands had gone home downhearted. The women did not know that their husbands had later returned to Chipping Norton and were part of the disturbance there. The women thought that the disturbance was made by the working people of the town and neighbourhood of Chipping Norton, who were furious at the outcome of the court case.

Forbes wrote that the women's story was told clearly, openly confirming many of the details without any bitterness, and that Mary Moss had added, with a sigh, 'I little thought I should ever see the inside of a prison, but if it does good for others I shan't trouble.' She then started to open a batch of letters that her husband had been saving while she was away.[11] However, a later report revealed that Elizabeth Pratley was still unwell and could hardly speak. Her throat and chest were very sore and her limbs ached.[12]

CHAPTER 13: RALLYING

CELEBRATIONS and REWARDS

The National Agricultural Labourers' Union arranged a rally and celebration for the women on the Ascott village green, so that they could present £5 to each of them in person. The rally was held on Friday 20 June. The union president, Joseph Arch, the Reverend Frederick Attenborough, and others arrived at Ascott station on the 5 p.m. train. They were met by the union secretary, Christopher Holloway, several other unionists, and fifteen of the sixteen women, all of whom were 'dressed in Union blue dresses, with head gear of a like colour'.[1] Elizabeth Pratley was still too unwell to attend. As Joseph Arch left the station platform, he was loudly cheered. He then walked with the women and the delegates to the Swan Inn, where tea was provided. The rally began shortly after 6 p.m.

According to a newspaper report, the village green 'presented quite a lively appearance, stalls, swings, etc., being erected thereon'.[2] Many years later, Mont Abbott from Enstone (about five miles northeast of Ascott-under-Wychwood) orally recorded memories of his 1870s childhood, including an account of a fair which would probably have been similar to the rally for the Ascott women. The excitement had started two days before, with the fun-fair rumbling in:

> It be all drawed and be worked by horses and manpower. Took two nights and a day to set up. The folks parleyed in a ring drawing lots for the different sites; us kids followed this important summit longin' them to get down to the real business of unloading the rides so's we could help, and lighting them camp fires so that we could smell the flash points of their roving life. Mr Glover be hard put to keep our noses to the grindstone all the next long day at school, prising us off the long low school wall; we clung like limpets looking over at the billowing tide of tarpaulin and waves of bunting rising up all the way up the main street.
>
> The pounding of mallets and the chink of chains, the shouts and whinnies of they great

fairground foreigners in our midst be all wild music to our Enstone ears. As soon as us kids left the school at 4 o'clock, the women of the village charged in bearing mops, brooms, buntings of Union Jack, buckets of wild flowers, baskets of grub. We'd dash off home and polish off our tea of roly poly pudding and clatter back kaping well out of earshot of our Mam's cry, 'Back by eight remember'. By nine they come searching for we. Most likely they cop us out in the dark field gazing at they fair folk... camped outside their lamp lit caravans. They come to scold, but stop to watch the slow twisting magic of those streams of cobweb sugar from the steaming cauldron below. Ha'past I'd be bedded down alongside my brothers in the moonlit attic it would seem the whole village was hushed lying in wait for the dawn ...[3]

Amidst all the activity on the Ascott green, a wagon was used as a platform for the speakers: Joseph Arch, Frederick Attenborough, Gabriel Banbury, Christopher Holloway, and Joseph Leggett. The weather was fine, and a large number of people, including Robert Hambidge, had gathered from Ascott and the neighbouring village.[4]

Christopher Holloway, as chairman, opened the proceedings, briefly stated the object of the meeting, and then called on Reverend Attenborough to speak. As Attenborough stood up, he was cheered loudly. He believed that the women did not break any laws that they were aware of, and they did not think they were doing anything wrong. He thought that the treatment they had received was quite outrageous, and he was determined to do something that should show them that there was one Christian man in England who thought that they were dealt with in an unchristian-like manner.

He had spoken with his friend Joseph Arch and they had agreed to send a letter to the newspapers, asking for subscriptions on behalf of the women. The letters had accordingly been sent to the *Daily News* and the *Birmingham Daily Post*, appealing for contributions. There had been a great response.[5]

Attenborough then read several letters he had received, expressing deep sympathy for the women. He said the list of subscribers to the fund was comprised of labouring men, women, tradesmen, magistrates, farmers, clergymen, and members of almost every profession, with the amounts ranging from tuppence farthing to £10. In addition to receiving letters from nearly every county in England, he had heard from France and Wales. In conclusion, he said he hoped the money he was about to give the women would be put to good use (a rather patronising comment). Each woman, in her union blue attire, came up to the wagon, one by one, to receive her money, no doubt to the acclamation of their supporters.

CELEBRATIONS and REWARDS

How did all the women come to be dressed in royal blue, the colour of the union, with matching 'head gear'? One story passed down over the years is that the union gave each woman enough silk to make a dress; another story holds that the union gave them each a blue dress and a matching blue bonnet. Twenty days had passed since the second group of seven women were released from prison—enough time for the dresses to be made, if this was well organised. It is possible that Mrs Leggett, the union secretary's wife, bought the material, but who cut out and sewed the dresses? The several women who made gloves for a living could have done the sewing, provided they had somewhere to do it. Elizabeth and Mary Pratley, for example, who lived in the old workhouse, had no table for cutting out the fabric or anywhere to sit and sew. Perhaps the local tailor and tailoress, William Dearing and his wife, Ann, made them, or Mary Lee, the sewing mistress at the school, may have helped. However the task was accomplished, it seems clear that all the women had new blue outfits for the meeting, paid for by the union.

When the union president, Joseph Arch, rose to speak, the crowd cheered. He ranged over a wide variety of subjects. He mentioned the cost of defending the agricultural labourers because of the unjust charges brought against them by magistrates. He spoke of the thousands of acres of non-productive land across the country used for the sport and pleasure of a few, when it could be cultivated and productive. He wanted suffrage of the people (that is, men) at the next election, the disestablishment of the Church of England, and the repeal of the Criminal Law Amendment Act, the Master and Servant Act, and the Game Laws. His ambition was to raise his fellow working men from their present position and promote the ongoing emigration of labourers.

Despite having barred women from joining the union, Arch knew their value as supporters, as he then appealed to them for their assistance in the cause. He asked his listeners to remember what the great William Wilberforce had said when they were trying to emancipate the slaves of the West Indies: 'Give me the sympathies of the women of England and I can liberate them in one year.'[6] Yet the fact that the women, too, were working people, and often farm labourers themselves, was ignored.

Banbury and Leggett briefly addressed the meeting, after which votes of thanks were unanimously accorded to the speakers and chairman. The proceedings ended with lusty cheers for the union and Mr Arch.[7]

CHAPTER 14: FUTURE IMPACT
THE WOMEN'S LEGACY

The actions of the sixteen women were to have far-reaching consequences for the labour movement, for the union, for the Liberal government of the day, and for the women themselves and their families. As historian and teacher Ralph Mann wrote, 'The story was a small step in women's emancipation. It was something which they achieved within the realm of trade unionism.'[1]

The women's actions and treatment, highlighted by the trial, the sentence, and the subsequent riot at the Chipping Norton police station, brought the National Agricultural Labourers' Union much welcome publicity and provided another clear example of discriminatory treatment of the labouring class. Together with the associated newspaper coverage, this resulted in a notable influx of new union members.

The case of the Ascott martyrs may also have been a factor influencing William Gladstone, leader of the Liberal government, in his decision to resign the following year. A general election followed in February 1874, and his political opponent, Benjamin Disraeli, became Prime Minister.

The women's ordeal undoubtedly helped to achieve a change in the law on picketing, which remains significant to this day. Disraeli's Conservative government subsequently repealed the Criminal Law Amendment Act of 1871, under which the magistrates had sentenced the women to prison. Picketing became legal with the passing of both the Conspiracy and Protection of Property Act 1875 and the Employers and Workmen Act 1875.

When the seven women serving ten days were released from prison and attended the large gathering in their honour in Chipping Norton, the idea of extending the franchise to all male householders was raised for the first time by the union leaders. During his term in government, Gladstone had suggested enfranchising the (male) farm labourer; opposition to this notion was highlighted as a factor leading to Disraeli being returned to power with a Conservative majority. It was another ten years before Gladstone, once again Prime Minister, extended the franchise to male agricultural labourers and other classes of men in the 1884 Reform Act. This gave the counties the same basis for the franchise as the boroughs—adult male householders and £10 lodgers—and added about six million to the total number of men who could vote in parliamentary elections.[2] Yet although the size of the electorate was widened considerably, 40 percent of adult men and all adult women still had no vote.[3]

The publicity created by the women's imprisonment and the reaction to it not only gave the National Agricultural Labourers' Union more opportunity to promote their cause; it also provided an effective platform for Joseph Arch to be seen as heading a successful movement, and provided him with many more opportunities to speak out against the inequalities between the rich and poor, and help the union to develop its policies. In 1884, the year that the franchise was extended, Joseph Arch was elected to Parliament as the Member for North-West Norfolk.

The women's case also encouraged those who questioned the wisdom of having clergymen as magistrates. From 1873 onwards, the clergy were discouraged from sitting on the Bench. Within twenty years this role had almost petered out, and by 1900 only forty clerical magistrates remained. Rather than upholding and enforcing public morality in the courts, the clergy's role became more centred on pastoral care.[4]

CHANGES to AGRICULTURE

Economic forces played a part in what happened to British farmers and farm labourers in the last quarter of the nineteenth century. While the National Agricultural Labourers' Union did later achieve a rise in wages from twelve to fourteen shillings a week, the golden years of agriculture had already passed. Disraeli had predicted in 1846 that agriculture would collapse when free trade was introduced, and it was ironic that he should have been in power when it happened. Cheaper rail transport in America and steam cargo ships on the Atlantic crossing brought Britain more affordable corn from America and Canada. Wheat prices also fell, and wool was imported from Australasia. From 1882, refrigerated ships were bringing in cheaper mutton from Australia and New Zealand.

Agriculture in England also suffered through a series of exceptionally wet, followed by exceptionally dry summers, resulting in poor harvests. Many cattle were infected with foot and mouth disease and pleura-pneumonia. Farmers found themselves caught between falling profits and rising wages, which resulted in a drop in their living standards. Over the years from 1875 to 1900, many switched from arable to pastoral farming.

EMIGRATION

The increasing mechanisation of agriculture fuelled emigration, with large numbers of farm labourers and their families moving to North America, Australia, and New Zealand. Four of the sixteen Ascott women were among them.

Elizabeth Pratley was the first to go: on 14 July, seven weeks after her release from prison. With her royal red flannel petticoat and five shillings, and her union blue, some say silk, dress and bonnet and £5, she and her husband Eli, with their three children, Elizabeth (4), Ellen (2), and eleven-month-old Eli, boarded the SS *Nyanza* in Plymouth for Canada. They reached Montreal in just over three weeks, on 5 August 1873.

Like all immigrants arriving in Canada, they would have stayed for a week or so in the quarantine barracks, 'a dockside complex built to house the newly arrived settlers, with free accommodation for a thousand people at a time, which included a separate women's wing with its own toilet facilities and ample laundry and cooking facilities'. When Joseph Arch visited the barracks, also known as the Emigrant's Home, about three weeks before the Pratley family arrived, he was extremely pleased with the accommodation provided. 'The women had a lofty wing set apart for their special use, there were admirable lavatories, there was a capital laundry, and ample cooking accommodation. Upstairs the large rooms were fitted with sloping sleeping benches ...'[5]

The Pratley family moved from the barracks to York, Toronto, where Elizabeth worked as a servant. But for her, the dream of a new and promising beginning was not fulfilled. Elizabeth never fully recovered from the chill she had caught on that cold, damp night when the women were taken to Oxford Gaol in the open drag. In her weakened state, probably during her stay in the barracks, she had caught what the authorities thought was typhoid, but was almost certainly typhus. On 26 September 1873, six weeks after their arrival in Canada, she died.[6]

After Elizabeth's death, Eli packed up his belongings and children and sailed back to England. When he returned to Ascott-under-Wychwood, he gave the family clothes (presumably including Elizabeth's) to his mother, Jemima, to wash. She became infected from this soiled laundry and died in December 1873 from what was then correctly identified as typhus. Little Eli caught it too, and died the following February.[7]

Eli then found work as a groom on the Nightingale farm in Bishampton, near Pershore, in the neighbouring county of Worcestershire. Relatives later told of a young, pretty, strong-minded cook, Jane Malins, who also worked there, and it was not long before she was attracted to the handsome new groom with a sad face. The two of them eloped back to Ascott and married in May 1874.

Three months later, the determined emigrant once again set off to a new country, this time New Zealand. The Pratley family were not the only ones to leave Ascott: the school log book reported that between 21 and 25 September: 'The school this week lost about eleven of its scholars through certain families of the parish emigrating to New Zealand'.

Eli, Jane, and Eli's three-year-old daughter, Ellen, sailed out of Plymouth on 25 September 1874 on the clipper ship *Crusader*. They reportedly said later that when they saw 'The Lizard' peninsula disappear, near the most southerly point of the British mainland, they knew they would never see their homeland again. After a 96-day voyage they landed in the New Zealand port of Lyttelton, near Christchurch, on New Year's Eve, 31 December 1874. They stayed in the immigrants' barracks in Addington for a few days, until Eli was found work in Temuka, 88 miles (142 km) south of Christchurch and about 9 miles (15 km) north of Timaru. They travelled southwards to set up their new home.

On the same ship was Eli's brother Frederick and his wife, Mary Pratley, several months pregnant with her seventh child, and their other six children. On the voyage, Mary gave birth to a baby girl who did not survive. They too settled in Temuka.

Fanny Honeybone and Jane Moss's brother Peter Honeybone was also on the *Crusader*. With his wife, Millicent, and their two sons, Thomas (8) and John (4), they settled in North Canterbury. Others on board were John and Caroline Tymms (later Timms) from Ascott-under-Wychwood, and their children: Ann (9), eight-year-old twins Mary and John Henry, William (6), Reuben (4), and one-year-old George.

Just over a month later, on 31 October, Amelia Moss with her husband, George, and daughter Julia set off from England on the clipper ship *Michael Angelo*. They arrived in Nelson, New Zealand, on 22 January 1875, and settled in nearby Stoke.

The last of the sixteen women to emigrate was Ann Moss, who went to the United States. By 1880, Ann (known as Annie), and her husband Caleb, a blacksmith, were living in the small town of Utica, in the Hinds County of Mississippi, where she was 'keeping house'. Next door was another English family: John Williams (30), a carpenter, his wife, Martha, and their four children, who were born in Mississippi.

EPILOGUE

KEEPING the STORY ALIVE

When several families, including those of Eli Pratley and his brother Frederick, left Ascott-under-Wychwood for New Zealand in 1874 on the *Crusader*, they took with them the story of the sixteen women. Those who attended the fiftieth reunion of the arrival of the *Crusader* in New Zealand heard it from the president of the Reunion Committee, John Timms (formerly Tymms). He had been only eight years old in 1873, but could remember parts of what had happened. His version of the events was later printed in *The Clipper Ship Crusader 1865–1910: Memories and Records of Over Fifty Years' Pioneering*.[1] It was not a very accurate account, but at least it was recorded.

Although two of Mary and Frederick Pratley's sons, George (62) and Frederick (60), attended that reunion, the story was never passed down through Eli Pratley's family. By the time a Pratley family reunion was held in 1991, the descendants of Frederick Pratley (with one 't') were convinced that they were not related to Eli Prattley (whose name had begun to be spelt with two 'ts' after he arrived in New Zealand). I was at that 1991 reunion, and keen to tell the women's story as I knew it then.

Until now, there has been no book focusing specifically on the women and their actions. A number of shorter accounts have appeared, often in connection with union activities and emigration. John Kibble, in his book *Charming Charlbury with its Nine Hamlets & Chipping Norton*[2] included two reports from *Jackson's Oxford Journal* regarding the sixteen women. One, published on 22 May 1873, covered the riot that erupted following the news that the women were going to be sent to prison. The other, published on 28 June 1873, reported the presentation of £5 to each of the women at an open-air meeting on the village green.[3] Kibble also gave a brief explanation of the women's actions.

In 1978, J.R. Hodgkins published a book about radicalism in Banburyshire, 1832–1945. *Over the Hills to Glory* included a chapter on the trials of the union and about what Joseph Arch called the 'shameful Chipping Norton affair'.[4] The story has also been recounted in Eileen Meades's *History of Chipping Norton* (1949),[5] Reginald Groves's *Sharpen the Sickle* (1949),[6] and *Joseph Arch 1826–1919, the Farm Workers' Leader*, by Pamela Horn (1971).[7] Articles include 'The Ascott Women', by R.M. Walton (1961),[8] and 'The Ascott Women', by Elizabeth Finn (1987).[9] Because the Ascott dispute is so famous in trade union annals, it is also recorded in several union histories.[10]

In 1981 historian Rollo Arnold published *The Farthest Promised Land: English Villagers, New Zealand Immigrants of the 1870s*.[11] Writing about Oxfordshire and Wychwood Forest, he described 'the changing fortunes of the English agricultural labourer, and more particularly... his Revolt of the Field'. He included an extensive, thoroughly researched account of the women's actions and their aftermath;[12] but apart from mentioning Mary and Elizabeth Pratley, in relation to their complaints about their treatment in prison, he treats the women as an undifferentiated and otherwise anonymous group.

While carrying out his research, Arnold stayed in Ascott-under-Wychwood for about six weeks. During that time he interviewed Doris Warner, who had lived in the village all her life. In 1964 she had included the story of the sixteen women in her personal memoir, which won that year's Oxfordshire Rural Community County Council competition for rural memoirs. She described it as 'the story... as told in the newspapers of the time', but does not specify which newspapers. 'Mr. Baylis of Oxford who was a Reader at the Bodleian Library kindly helped me a great deal by obtaining a copy of newspapers of the time so I was able to get all the details correct.'[13] However, this was not quite accurate. Doris was particularly interested in keeping the Ascott martyrs' story alive because at least seven of the sixteen women were on her own family tree—and she had collected accounts from the 'old folks'. Fanny Honeybone, the last of the women who had been directly involved, died in 1939. It is possible that Doris interviewed

Fanny and recorded her first-hand experience of what happened. When interviewed for an article in *The Land Worker* in 1928, Fanny said:

> During the strike, Mr Hambridge [sic], the farmer, had sent two men to finish his pea hoeing,[14] and the women, including myself, went up the Ascot road to stop them. There was something of the idea of fun in what we did—certainly no intention to harm them. I got ten days, second division, in Oxford Gaol. I remember the coaches which met us and the demonstration afterwards in the Town Hall[15] at Chipping Norton. Those were stirring times and it gives me a thrill of pleasure to remember them.[16]

The other accounts Doris collected would probably have been second-hand, drawing largely on village memories. She was about 33 years old when her own grandmother Eleanor died, so had probably listened to her stories about the women. From those stories, as well as her memoir, Doris Warner wrote her play called *Over the Hills to Glory* (1953).

Three of the women mentioned in the play were among those imprisoned: 'Becky' (Rebecca Smith), 'Levia' (Levia Dring), and 'Nellie Pratley' (Ellen Pratley). Doris's grandmother, Eleanor Honeybone, and her daughter Fanny also have large parts; but this Fanny Honeybone, who was related to Doris, was *not* the one who was imprisoned. That Fanny was the daughter of John and Jane Honeybone, who were unrelated to Eleanor or Doris. In 1873, Doris's mother, Kate, was about three years old, and Kate's sister Jane was about seven. Yet in the play, Jane is portrayed as Fanny's Aunt Jane, although she was in fact Doris's aunt. As well as Doris Warner's play, a musical documentary, *The Ascott Martyrs*, was performed in Chipping Norton by the Spring Street Theatre Company, 16–18 June 1982.

Eric Moss, grandson of Walter Moss and second cousin of Doris, also lived in Ascott-under-Wychwood for most of his life. Seven of the sixteen women were also on his family tree: Jane Honeybone, young Mary Moss (otherwise Smith), Mary Moss, Caroline Moss, Charlotte Moss, Amelia Moss, and Anne Moss. In 1999 Eric Moss wrote *Walk Humble, My Son*,[17] a book about his life in the village. One page, headed 'The Ascott Martyrs', explains what the women did and their resulting punishment.[18]

Ralph Mann, a former history teacher and later a parish vicar, also kept the story alive, and became known as the leading authority on the Ascott martyrs. He set out to write his own book about them, but, sadly, did not complete it before he died. He gave many talks and several newspaper interviews about the women. When Jock Phillips, the Chief Historian for the then Historical

Branch of the New Zealand Department of Internal Affairs, was in England in April 1997, he recorded an interview with Ralph Mann, including a description of the Wychwood area, an account of the actions of the Ascott martyrs and their aftermath, and migration away from the village.[19]

In 1996 came an impressive novel, *Riding to Jerusalem* by Elspeth Sandys.[20] It deals with the repression of early unionism in the nineteenth-century Cotswolds and how the 'white slaves of England' eventually emigrated to New Zealand. Sandys, now based in New Zealand, had lived in Ascott-under-Wychwood for ten years; there she heard many stories, which, she says, 'lie at the heart of *Riding to Jerusalem*'.[21] It includes a fictionalised account of the Ascott martyrs and their exploits.

And today, perhaps the most effective commemoration of the sixteen women themselves comes in the form of the tree and seat with their names that stands on the village green in Ascott-under-Wychwood.

It is hoped that this book will take its place alongside others about women's protest movements, trade union activity and emigration. Today there are also a number of websites dealing with their story, including my own, created in 1997 and since updated.[22]

The new seat around the horse chestnut on the village green.
(Sue Matthews, Abingdon, Oxfordshire UK.)

BIOGRAPHIES
THE SIXTEEN WOMEN WHO WERE SENT TO PRISON

LEVIA DRING (Lavinia, née Moss) 1828–1908
OXFORD PRISON CHARGE SHEET RECORD MAY 1873
Name: Lavinia Dring; Married; **Age** 44. **Born:** [1828] Ascott-under-Wychwood.
Residence: Ascott-under-Wychwood. **Occupation:** gloveress. **Religion:** Baptist.
Sentence: 7 days with hard labour.

Levia Dring's name was on the original wooden seat built around the horse chestnut tree on the village green in Ascott-under-Wychwood. On the charge sheet she was recorded as Lavinia Dring although she seems to have been commonly known as Levia, which was in fact her baptismal name.

Levia was related to six of the other women. She was sister-in-law to Amelia Moss and Ann Susan Moss, aunt by marriage to Elizabeth and Mary Pratley, great-aunt by marriage to Ellen Pratley, and cousin by marriage to Charlotte Moss.

Levia was baptised on 26 October 1828 in Ascott-under-Wychwood, the daughter of William Moss (son of Elizabeth Thornett and George Moss) and his second wife Hannah Lardner (née Busby). William's first wife, Jane, had died aged 35, a few days after giving birth to a baby girl, Jane Elizabeth, who died two weeks later. William was left with four children under ten years of age. Six months after his wife's death William married Hannah, whose first husband had died four years earlier.

Levia was William and Hannah's second child; their firstborn, Philip, died two months before Levia was baptised. She had three half-sisters: Jemima (13), Hannah (11), and Mary (9), and one half-brother, William, aged six. Her younger brothers were George, born 1830; Joseph, 1833; and John, 1839. Her little sister Emma, born 1835, died two years later.

By the time the 1841 census was taken, Levia (12) was living at home with her parents and three of her brothers: George (10), Joseph (7), and John (2). In 1851 Levia, aged 22, was still living at home and working as a gloveress. Her father, William, and her other brothers, George (20), Joseph (17) and John (11), were all farm labourers.

Levia was about 27 years old when she married James Dring, the son of Samuel and Hannah Dring. James was an agricultural labourer, also born in Ascott-under-Wychwood. They married on 23 July 1855 in the village. Witnesses at the wedding were Joseph Moss (Levia's brother) and Amelia Moss (grand-daughter of William Moss and Susannah Scarsebrook). Amelia married Levia's brother George Moss the next year, 1856.

Also in 1856, Levia and James's first daughter, Emma Sophie, was born. Annie Maria arrived two years later in 1858, followed by Mary Jane (1860) and Alice Eva (1862). In 1871, Levia and James lived close to Crown Farm in Ascott-under-Wychwood with their four daughters. Her mother had died a year earlier, in 1872. Her father was 83, making him one of the oldest men in Ascott. Since Levia's father, husband, and brothers were all agricultural labourers, they were probably all on strike, which gave her good reason to be involved in the women's actions.

Other family members living in the village were her brother George (42) and his wife Amelia (who was also sent to prison) and their daughter Julia. They had moved to Ascott from the nearby village of Shipton-under-Wychwood some time in the previous two years.

Another brother, Joseph (39), and his wife, Hannah, lived in the Turnpike house in Ascott with their six children: George (13), William (12), Albert (10), Charles (6), Samuel (4), and Emma (3). Her youngest brother, John (34), was married to Susannah Owen, born in Chipping Norton in 1845, and they were living in Ascott. Susannah may well have been Ann Susan Moss, one of the sixteen women imprisoned, as their ages almost matched and their birthplaces were the same.

Levia's half-sister Jemima Pratley was my great-great-grandmother. She was the only one of the offspring of her father's first marriage living in Ascott at that time. Jemima (58) had been a widow for nine years and worked as a charwoman. She lived with her youngest son, Charles (15). Two of Jemima's other sons—Frederick and my great-grandfather Eli Pratley—were married with children and also lived in the village. Jemima's stepson John and his wife Jane Moss from Leafield, were also living in the village with their seven children.

Levia's daughter Emma married Nathan Cooper, a mason's labourer, on 9 November 1878. In 1881 they were living in Shorthampton, a nearby hamlet between Charlbury and Ascott-under-Wychwood, with one-year-old Alice. Also in their household was Emma's sister Mary (21). Emma and Mary both worked as gloveresses.

In 1881 Levia (her name is recorded as Lavinia) and her husband, James, were living near the Swan Inn. Their other two daughters, Ann (Annie) Maria (23), and Alice (19), both unmarried, lived and worked at Ringwood House, a farm of 800 acres at Minster Lovell in Oxfordshire, run by Robert Abraham, who also employed eighteen men and twelve boys.

Six years later Levia's husband, James, died, and was buried on 28 March 1887 in Ascott-under-Wychwood. Her daughter Ann (31) married William Mildenhall (27), a labourer, on 5 October 1890. By the time their first child, Ernest William, was born, they were living in Marylebone, London.

In the 1891 census, Levia (62) was living with her third daughter Mary (31) and her granddaughter Alice Cooper (11) in Chapel Yard, Ascott-under-Wychwood. Mary was working as a gloveress and Alice was a schoolgirl. Alice's parents (Levia's daughter Emma and her husband Nathan Cooper) were still living in Shorthampton with their two boys, Nathan (9) and one-year-old James. Levia's youngest daughter Alice married John Medlicott on 16 April 1892, two years after they had both been witnesses at Ann and William Mildenhall's marriage.

In 1901 Levia was still living in Chapel Yard with her daughter Mary (who was known as Aunt Polly, and apparently had a club foot.[1]) and they were both gloveresses. Alice (21) was living there too, and working as a domestic cook.

Levia died on 7 December 1908 in the village where she had lived all her life. The parish burial register records her as Levia Dring, aged 80.

FANNY HONEYBONE (later Fanny Rathband) 1857–1939

OXFORD PRISON CHARGE SHEET RECORD MAY 1873
Name: Fanny Honeybone; Unmarried; Age 16. **Born:** [1857] Ascott-under-Wychwood. **Residence:** Ascott-under-Wychwood. **Occupation:** gloveress. **Religion:** Baptist. **Sentence:** 10 days with hard labour.

Fanny Honeybone's name was on the original wooden seat, and was also on the charge sheet. Aged only sixteen in 1873, she was the youngest woman to be sentenced.

Fanny was related to three of the other women. She was Jane Moss's sister, and a cousin by marriage of Rebecca Smith and Martha Smith.

Fanny was the daughter of John Honeybone from Ascott-under-Wychwood and Jane Newman from nearby Langley. She was baptised on 19 July 1857 in Ascott-under-Wychwood, the youngest of eleven children. In 1871, she was a domestic servant living and working in the Churchill Arms public house.

Three years after her imprisonment, on 9 September 1876, 19-year-old Fanny married Edwin Rathband, an agricultural labourer, and they lived in Hawks Yard, Milton-under-Wychwood. Between 1876 and 1901, Fanny gave birth to fourteen children, at least five of whom died in infancy or childhood.

By the time of the 1881 census, they had three children: Jane (4), Ada (2), and eleven-month-old George. Jane died later that same year and was buried in the village on 4 May 1881.

At the 1891 census, Fanny and Edwin were still in Hawks Yard, together with their children: Ada (12), George (10), Frank (7), Ruben (6), Millicent (4) and two-year-old Lizzie. All except the two youngest children attended school.

Six years later, in July 1897, three of Fanny's children died. Seven-month-old Wilfred John was buried on 11 July, Alice (4) was buried on 20 July, and Ruben (12) was buried on 24 July. The cause of their deaths is unknown, but there was an influenza epidemic in England at that time.[2] The following year, Fanny's two-week-old baby, Lily Mabel, died and was buried on 16 February 1898.

At the 1901 census Fanny and Edwin, now a mason's labourer, were still living in Hawks Yard with Lizzie (12), Harry (9), Ida (5), Herbert (2), and a one-month-old baby.

In later life, Fanny said she was 'proud to be the last surviving woman of the sixteen women who suffered the penalty of the law for the cause of the agricultural labourers ...' She recalled:

> During the strike, Mr Hambridge [sic], the farmer, had sent for two men to finish his pea hoeing,[3] and the women, including myself, went up the Ascott-under-Wychwood road to stop them. There was something of the idea of fun in what we did—certainly no intention to harm them. I got ten days, second division, in Oxford Gaol. I remember the coaches which met us and the demonstration afterwards in the Town Hall at Chipping Norton. Those were stirring times and it gives me a thrill of pleasure to remember them.[4]

Fanny Rathband (née Honeybone) in later years. (Image supplied by Janet Wiltshire, Milton-under-Wychwood, Oxfordshire, UK.)

Fanny Rathband died in 1939 at the age of 81 years.

AMELIA MOSS (née Moss) 1836–1918

OXFORD PRISON CHARGE SHEET RECORD MAY 1873
Name: Amelia Moss; Married; **Age** 36. **Born**: [1836] Ascott-under-Wychwood.
Residence: Ascott-under-Wychwood. **Occupation**: gloveress.
Religion: Baptist. **Sentence**: 7 days with hard labour.

Amelia Moss was not named on the original seat, but her name was on the charge sheet, and she was sentenced to seven days in prison with hard labour.

Amelia was related to nine of the other women. She was Charlotte Moss's sister, sister-in-law to Levia Dring and Martha Moss, cousin to Caroline

Moss, cousin by marriage to Ann Moss, Mary Moss, Jane Moss, and Ann Susan (Susannah) Moss, and cousin by marriage once removed to Mary Moss (Smith).

Amelia was the sixth and last surviving child of James Moss, son of William Moss and Susannah Scarsebrook, and his first wife, Charlotte Hancock. She was baptised Frances Amelia on 19 June 1836 in Ascott-under-Wychwood. James and Charlotte's seventh child, Jason, was born two years later, but neither he nor his mother survived, and both were buried on 5 August 1838 in Ascott.

Two years after Charlotte died, James married Mary Ann Bayliss from Ramsden on 5 November 1840. Together they had ten children. James fathered 17 children altogether.

In the 1841 census Amelia (4) lived with her father, a sawyer; her stepmother; her brothers, George (14), William (12) and Alfred (6), and her sister, seven-year-old Charlotte.

In 1851 Amelia, then 15, lived at home with her father, stepmother, three brothers, and a sister, as well as three half-brothers: Jason (8), Jesse (6), and James Charles (4), and a half-sister, one-year-old Thirza. Her father and older brothers were sawyers.

Five years later, aged 20, Amelia married George Moss, on 15 October 1856 in Ascott-under-Wychwood. George was Levia Dring's brother, and the grandson of George Moss and Elizabeth Thornett.

In 1861 George and Amelia were living in Ascott-under-Wychwood. Their daughter Julia was born in 1870. In 1871 the family was living in Shipton-under-Wychwood, but by 1873 they were back in Ascott.

On 31 October 1874, a year after Amelia went to prison, the family emigrated on the clipper ship *Michael Angelo*. They arrived in Nelson, New Zealand, on 22 January 1875.

Four days before the ship berthed at the Port of Nelson, the ship's captain, Mackenzie Luckie, died from heart disease. Mr Esson, the chief officer, found himself in the great Pacific Ocean, not only in charge of the ship, but with the safety of about 340 souls in his hands, and this after being almost three months at sea without sighting any land. Mr Esson carefully navigated the ship through many intricate windings from the end of the sandspit to the lighthouse on the Boulder Bank during the dark hours of a hazy night, where he brought her with her living freight safely to anchor.[5]

In 1890, Amelia and George, working as a labourer, were living in Stoke, Nelson. Their daughter Julia, aged 24, married William Stewart, also 24, on 23 March 1894 at her home. William was an engineer, and the son of James Stewart and Mary Ann Robertson.

Amelia's husband, George, died in 1917 at the age of 86. Amelia died in Wanganui, where her daughter lived, the following year aged 83, and was buried on 2 August 1918 in Aramoho Cemetery, Wanganui.

ANN MOSS (née Hudson) 1845– ?

OXFORD PRISON CHARGE SHEET RECORD MAY 1873
Name: Ann Moss; Married; Age 22. **Born:** [1845] Sutton, Stanton Harcourt.
Residence: Ascott-under-Wychwood. **Occupation:** labourer [farm labourer].
Religion: Church of England. **Sentence:** 10 days with hard labour.

On the original wooden seat, Ann Moss was recorded as Mrs Caleb Moss. However, she was charged and sentenced as Ann Moss.

Ann was related by marriage to seven of the other women. She was a cousin by marriage to Amelia, Charlotte, Caroline, Mary, Martha, and Jane Moss, and cousin by marriage once removed to Mary Moss (Smith).

The daughter of Thomas Hudson and Eliza White, Ann was baptised on 5 September 1845, in the hamlet of Sutton, in the parish of Stanton Harcourt, about 12 miles east of Ascott-under-Wychwood, and just over six miles west of Oxford.

In 1861, eight-year-old Ann was living with her parents, her half-sister Priscilla (16), her sister Sarah (2), and her brothers, George (6) and baby Henry. By 1871 Ann (18) was working as a domestic and general servant for James Goatley (30), farmer of 100 acres, and his sister Sarah (27), in Ramsden. James also employed two men and two boys.

Ann married Caleb Moss on 6 February 1873 in Eynsham, Oxfordshire. Caleb was the eleventh of twelve children born to George Moss, son of William Moss and Susannah Scarsebrook, and Esther Westbury, from Ascott-under-Wychwood. Two years earlier in 1871, Caleb, aged 19, had been living at home with his parents and working as an agricultural labourer. Also living there were his sister-in-law Jane, wife of his brother Jason, and their seven-year-old daughter, Ann, who was born in South Africa. Caleb's eldest sister, Jane, was married to John Pratley, half-brother of Eli and Frederick Pratley.

By 1880 Ann, known as Annie, and Caleb, now a blacksmith, were living in the small town of Utica, in the Hinds County of Mississippi, United States of America. She was recorded as 'keeping house'.[6] They were living next door to English-born John Williams (30), a carpenter, and his wife Martha (30). John and Martha had four children who were born in Mississippi.

ANN SUSAN MOSS (née Owen?) 1846– before 1881

OXFORD PRISON CHARGE SHEET RECORD MAY 1873
Name: Ann Susan Moss; Married; Age 25. **Born:** [1846] Chipping Norton.
Residence: Ascott-under-Wychwood. **Occupation:** labourer [field worker].
Religion: Church of England. **Sentence:** 10 days with hard labour.

The name Ann Susan Moss was not on the original wooden seat, but it was on the charge sheet.

If, as seems likely, Ann Susan was actually Susannah Moss, she was related to six of the other women. She was sister-in-law to Levia Dring and Amelia Moss, aunt by marriage to Mary and Elizabeth Pratley, great aunt by marriage to Ellen Pratley, and cousin by marriage to Charlotte Moss.

Tracing Ann Susan proved to be more of a challenge than was the case with the other women. The nearest match was Susannah Owen, who was born in Dunthrop, near Chipping Norton, to Edward Owen of Swerford, an agricultural labourer, and Mary Taylor of Lower Heyford. Susannah was baptised 17 May 1846 in Dunthrop; this would make her 27 years old, rather than 25, in 1873.

The hamlet of Dunthrop is in the parish of Heythrop, about a mile away from Swerford, a small village on the River Swere in the Cotswold Hills, roughly four miles northeast of Chipping Norton. Lower Heyford is a village beside the River Cherwell, about 12 miles east of Chipping Norton and six miles west of Bicester, a market town. One of the magistrates who conducted the case against the women, Thomas Harris, was the Rector of Swerford, and probably knew the Owen family, since they belonged to the Church of England.

In 1851 four-year-old Susannah was living with her parents and two-year-old sister Charlotte, in Heythrop. Her father, Edward, was an agricultural labourer. In 1861, Susannah (15), was still at home in Heythrop with her parents, her sister Rebecca (6), and her brothers Thomas (10), Frederick (3), and six-month-old John.

She married Levia Dring's brother, John Moss, on 8 September 1866 in Ascott-under-Wychwood. It is not known where they were living in 1871. Levia Dring and Amelia Moss were Susannah's sisters-in-law, making it more than likely that she was involved in the picketing dispute, whether she was indeed Ann Susan or not.

The identity of the Ann Susan, who appears on the charge sheet, is a mystery. Some of the other women who went to prison had nicknames. For example, Mary Pratley was known as Polly, Ellen Pratley was known as Nelly, Amelia was probably Milly, Ann Moss was later known as Annie, Caroline Moss was probably Carrie, Charlotte Moss was probably Lottie, Elizabeth Pratley was called Betty, and Rebecca Smith, Becky.

What happened to Ann Susan/Susannah after 1873 is unknown, but she may well have died. In the 1881 census, her husband, John Moss, aged 40, was recorded as being an unmarried lodger in the household of Philip Long (71), a carpenter, and his wife, Eleanor (67), in Handborough, Oxford. Also lodging there was Martha Moss's husband, William (49), and the two of them were working as railway plate layers.

At some time after 1881, John married Emma Wright, whose husband, James, had died the previous year. Emma had been a witness for the women at the trial.

CAROLINE MOSS (later Caroline Phillips) 1856–1875

OXFORD PRISON CHARGE SHEET RECORD MAY 1873
Name: Caroline Moss; Single; Age 18. **Born:** [1856] Ascott-under-Wychwood.
Residence: Ascott-under-Wychwood. **Occupation:** gloveress.
Religion: Church of England. **Sentence:** 7 days with hard labour.

Caroline Moss was named on the original seat and on the charge sheet.

Caroline was related to seven of the other women. She was sister-in law to Mary Moss, first cousin to Charlotte and Amelia Moss, and cousin by marriage to Jane Moss, Ann Moss, and Martha Moss. She was also cousin by marriage, once removed, to young Mary Moss (Smith).

Caroline, baptised 19 October 1856 in Ascott-under-Wychwood, was the eleventh and youngest child of Joseph Moss and his second wife, Ann Pratley from Leafield. Her father was the son of William Moss and Susannah Scarsebrook. He was widowed for the second time two years later, when Anne died. She was buried on 25 July 1858.

In 1861 four-year-old Caroline was living with her father, Joseph, a wheelwright, her brother Charles (24), an agricultural labourer, her sisters Harriet (16), and Emma (14), and her brother Joshua (7).

In 1871 Caroline was recorded in the census as aged 16, and a domestic servant in the household of Thomas Kerwood (26) and his wife, Mary (22). Thomas was farming 67 acres at Woodstock Road, St Giles, Summertown, Oxfordshire, and also employed three men.

By 1873 Caroline had moved back to Ascott-under-Wychwood. In 1874, she married Thomas Phillips, a farm labourer, in Shipton-under-Wychwood, Oxfordshire. But that marriage did not last long, as Caroline died in 1875 in Shipton-under-Wychwood, aged just 20.

In the 1881 census, Thomas Phillips was living with his new wife, Eliza, and adopted daughter, Eliza Turner, at Coldstone Farm in Shipton-under-Wychwood.

CHARLOTTE MOSS (née Moss) 1833–1904

OXFORD PRISON CHARGE SHEET RECORD MAY 1873
Name: Charlotte Moss; Married; Age 39. **Born:** [1833] Ascott-under-Wychwood.
Residence: Ascott-under-Wychwood. **Occupation:** labourer (field worker).
Religion: Church of England. **Sentence:** 10 days with hard labour.

Charlotte Moss was named on the original seat and on the charge sheet.

Charlotte was related to nine of the other women. She was sister to Amelia Moss, sister-in-law to Martha Moss, cousin to Caroline Moss, cousin by marriage to Ann Moss, Mary Moss, Jane Moss, Levia Dring, and Ann Susan (Susannah) Moss, and cousin by marriage once removed to Mary Moss (Smith).

BIOGRAPHIES

The daughter of James Moss and Charlotte Hancock, she was baptised on 24 February 1833 in Ascott-under-Wychwood. When she was five years old her mother died and was buried on 5 August 1838.

In 1841 Charlotte was living in Church Street with her father James, a sawyer; her stepmother Ann (Mary Ann Bayliss), three brothers: George (14), William (12), and six-year-old Alfred; and her four-year-old sister Amelia.

In 1851 Charlotte, then 18, and her sister, 15-year-old Amelia, were working as gloveresses. With their parents, they were part of a large family of eleven, living in a cottage on Church Street. Charlotte's brothers George (25), William (23), and Alfred (17) were all sawyers. The family included her three half-brothers, Jason (8), Jesse (6), James (4), and her one-year-old half-sister, Thirza.

Charlotte Moss married William Moss on 25 May 1854 in Ascott-under-Wychwood. Surprisingly, they were unrelated. Charlotte's paternal grandparents were William Moss and Susannah Scarsebrook. William's paternal grandparents were George Moss and Elizabeth Thornett, and his maternal grandparents were Benjamin Moss and Mary Jackson.

In 1861 Charlotte and William lived in a cottage near the Swan Inn, with her brother Will (Martha Moss's husband), aged 33, a sawyer, as well as her half-brother Reuben (8). Two lodgers, Charles Lansbury (18), a milk boy, and David Edgeworth (25), a carter, also resided in the cottage. Charlotte was a gloveress and William an agricultural labourer.

Charlotte and William had a son in 1863, also called William. When the next census was taken in 1871, Charlotte's husband was a railway servant.

In 1881 Charlotte was still a gloveress. Her husband was again a labourer, but their 18-year-old son, William, was working as a railway porter. A six-year-old niece, Clara Moss, whose mother had died, also lived with them at Mill Lane in Ascott-under-Wychwood.

Charlotte's son, William, married Alice Kench in September 1884. Over the next ten years they had at least five children. William, who continued to work for the railway, was one of Ascott-under-Wychwood's first Parish Councillors.[7]

In the 1891 census, Charlotte and her husband William, now a railway labourer, were still living in Mill Lane. Unfortunately, in July 1896, their son, William, fell while lighting one of the signal lamps on the railway station, and later died of his injuries.[8] Harry Honeybone recalled William as a decent fellow, he was a signal man with good wages, married to a nice woman from Charlbury, lived happy for a time but frequented the public house. Often, after a time of boozing and gambling, he became a physical wreck. Until one day, he went to the distant signal to put in the lamps and somehow fell from the lamp platform; no-one saw it happen but he was found there and they could only surmise as to what happened.[9]

When William was killed, his wife, Alice, was left with a young family to care for: Frederick (11), Reuben (9), Albert (8), Annie (3), and baby Alfred.

The 1901 census recorded Alice as living in a cottage with four of her children: Frederick (16), Albert (13), Annie (8), and Alfred (5). Alice worked as a laundress at home. In the same census, Reuben (14) was living with his maternal grandmother Ann Kench, and his aunt Annie Kench. They too worked as laundresses at home, in Sheep Street, Charlbury. Later Reuben fought in World War I and was awarded a Military Medal.[10]

In the 1901 census, Charlotte and William, a retired railway 'navvy', were still living in Mill Lane, Ascott. Charlotte died at the age of 71 and was buried on 2 September 1904 in Ascott-under-Wychwood, where she had lived all her life.

JANE MOSS (née Honeybone) 1842– ?

OXFORD PRISON CHARGE SHEET RECORD MAY 1873
Name: Jane Moss; Married; Age 31. **Born:** [1842] Ascott-under-Wychwood.
Residence: Ascott-under-Wychwood. **Occupation:** gloveress.
Religion: Baptist. **Sentence:** 7 days with hard labour.

The name of Jane Moss was not on the original wooden seat, but it was on the charge sheet. Jane was related to nine of the other women. She was Fanny Honeybone's sister, aunt by marriage to Mary Moss (otherwise Smith), and cousin by marriage to Mary Moss, Caroline Moss, Charlotte Moss, Amelia Moss, Ann Moss, Rebecca Smith, and Martha Smith.

Jane was the fourth child of John Honeybone from Ascott-under-Wychwood and Jane Newman from Langley. She was baptised on 20 February 1842 in Ascott-under-Wychwood.

BIOGRAPHIES

In 1851, nine-year-old Jane was living in a cottage on Lower Street with her parents, three sisters: Eliza (14), Ann (11) and Ellen (3), and three brothers: George (16), Peter (9), and Thomas (8). Her parents and her brother George were all farm labourers, and Eliza[11] was a gloveress. Jane and Peter were at school, while Ann stayed at home with Ellen and Thomas. The next year Jane's newly-born sister, Martha, died a fortnight after she was baptised, and was buried on 28 October 1852. Twins, Emma and Reuban, were born two years later, but only Reuban survived.

It is hard to imagine nine people living in their small cottage with a thatched roof. Twenty years later Jane's nephew, Harry Honeybone, went to live with his grandmother after his father, George, and his mother, Jane, died within six weeks of each other. He recalled that the cottage

> stands flush up to the road facing west; it stands on rising ground, there being three steps from the ground to the floor of the cottage. A third of the south end of the interior is partitioned off by a wooden partition. This portion is used as a scullery and pantry.[12]

At the north end was a wide fireplace with a recess at one side where two people could sit. He remembered his grandfather, John Honeybone, sitting by the fire, wearing the traditional smock frock, and 'smoking his clay pipe upside down, he had no teeth wherewith to hold it the right way up. He used to get spills of paper or poke a red hot coke from the fire onto his pipe to light it.'[13]

There was a staircase leading up to the bedrooms on the other side of the fireplace. Anyone wanting to reach the far bedroom had to pass through the first one, as it was partitioned in a similar way to the room below. The house was simply a shell with partitions. The birds used to make their nests in the thatch in the summer season and many times sparrows and starlings found their way into the bedrooms.[14]

By the time the 1861 census was taken, though two of the girls had married and moved away, eight people were still living in the cottage. Jane, a gloveress, and her baby son, George, were living at home with her father, John, a carter, and her mother, Jane. Also living in the cottage were her brothers George (26) a cowman, Thomas (11) a ploughboy, Reuban (6), and her three-year-old sister Fanny. Jane's brother 17-year-old Peter, an agricultural labourer, was lodging with his sister Eliza and her husband, John Sirman, in Langley. Another of Jane's sisters, Ellen (13), was staying with her aunt and uncle, Mary and Thomas Tymms, in Ascott-under-Wychwood.

Jane's sister Ann married Thomas Rainbow in 1858 and they lived in Shipton-under-Wychwood. Four years later, on 1 March 1862, Jane married Robert Moss, a shepherd, son of Thomas Moss and Ann Wiggins. Thomas was the son of William Moss and Susannah Scarsebrook.

In 1871 Jane, Robert, and their eleven-year-old son, George, were living at one end of the village; at the other end were Jane's mother (also called Jane), father John, and brother Thomas, both agricultural labourers.

In the late 1870s Jane's parents lost three of their children. In 1878 their eldest son George (43) and his wife (another Jane) died within six weeks of each other. Jane died in January 1879, aged 37, just six years after her imprisonment, and Ann (wife of Thomas Rainbow), died the same year in August, aged 39.

At the time of the 1881 census, Jane's husband, Robert, a widower, was a farm labourer lodging in Ascott-under-Wychwood with his brother Thomas, a hauler, and Thomas's wife, Eliza, a gloveress. Also in the house were their 18-year-old son Thomas, their daughter Jane (10), and Ann Smith (5), who was visiting. Eliza's daughter Mary was the young Mary Moss (otherwise known as Smith) who was sent to prison with the other women.

In the same 1881 census, Jane's son George, aged 20, was living in Long Handborough, Oxford, where he worked as a railway labourer. He was staying with William and Emma Walker and their two sons, William (24) and Frank (18), who with their father were blacksmiths. Also staying with the Walkers were William Harris (24) and George Evans (23), also railway labourers.

MARTHA MOSS (née Baylis) 1837–1882

OXFORD PRISON CHARGE SHEET RECORD MAY 1873
Name: Martha Moss; Married; Age 33 [she was actually 36]. **Born:** [1837] Mixbury, Oxfordshire. **Residence:** Ascott-under-Wychwood. **Occupation:** gloveress. **Religion:** Church of England. **Sentence:** 7 days with hard labour.

On the wooden seat around the tree, Martha Moss was named as Mrs William Moss, but she was Martha Moss on the charge sheet.

Martha was related to eight of the other women. She was the sister-in-law of Charlotte Moss, Amelia Moss, and Levia Dring; cousin by marriage

BIOGRAPHIES

to Jane, Mary, Caroline, and Ann Moss; and first cousin by marriage once removed to young Mary Moss (Smith).

The third child and only daughter of John Baylis of Mixbury, and Ann Taylor from nearby Finmere, Oxfordshire, Martha was born on 12 March 1837, and baptised on 3 December 1837 in the North Oxfordshire village of Mixbury. She was born four months after her two-year-old brother Joseph died from burns.

In 1841 four-year-old Martha was living at home with her parents and two brothers, William (8) and Josiah (2). Her father was an agricultural labourer. Ten years later Martha, aged 14, was still living at home with her parents and her three brothers, William (18), now an agricultural labourer, Josiah (12), and John (9).

Martha married William Moss, a sawyer and the brother of Charlotte Moss, in Over Norton, Oxfordshire, on 21 December 1857. William was cousin to Jane Moss's husband Robert, and cousin once removed to their son, George Moss, who was also working in Handborough. But in the 1861 census, although Martha (25) was recorded as married and the wife of a sawyer, she was living at 4 Cherwell Street, Banbury. Lodging at the same address was James Butler (23), a sawyer from Worcester. Martha's husband, William, known as Will, was living with his sister, Charlotte, and her family back in Ascott-under-Wychwood.

In the 1871 census, Martha and William Moss were lodging with Philip Pratley, his wife Jane (who was summonsed, but found not guilty), and their daughter Sarah, who was thirteen months old. Jane was a cousin once removed of Martha's husband.

By the 1881 census, it seems that Martha and William had separated, as Martha was living in Ascott-under-Wychwood and recorded as head of the household. Visiting with Martha on census night was Robert Morris, his wife, Mary, and their two children Frank (4) and nine-month-old Mary. Twenty years previously, Robert (then 15) had been a waiter in the Churchill Arms hotel in Ascott-under-Wychwood, where his father was the innkeeper.

In the same census, William Moss was working as a railway plate layer, lodging with 71-year-old Philip Long, a carpenter, and his 67-year-old wife Eleanor, in the village of Handborough, between Witney and Woodstock, Oxfordshire. Also lodging there was Levia Dring's brother John Moss, who also worked as a railway plate layer.

In 1882 Martha returned to Mixbury, Oxfordshire. She died at the age of 43, and was buried in Mixbury where she was born.

In the 1891 census, her husband, William, was an agricultural labourer living in a shed next to Vine Cottage where Ernest Bradford lived, in Ascott-under-Wychwood. In the 1901 census, he was an inmate in the Chipping Norton Union Workhouse as were three others from Ascott-under-Wychwood: William Smith, single (76), a farm labourer; Susannah Louise Smith, single (68), a glove finisher; and Henry Pratley, single (18), a coal miner. Henry was George and Mary Pratley's fifth child. Mary was the young Mary Moss (otherwise Smith) who was sent to prison with the Ascott women; she had died eleven years earlier, in 1890. Two other Pratley boys, although not obviously related to Henry, were in the workhouse at the same time. They were Charles (11) and Thomas (9) from the Oxfordshire village of Chadlington. Why the boys ended up in the workhouse is unknown. Historian Peter Higginbotham writes:

> People went for a variety of reasons. Usually, it was because they were too poor, old or ill to support themselves. This may have resulted from such things as a lack of work during periods of high unemployment, or someone having no family willing or able to provide care for them when they became elderly or sick. Unmarried pregnant women were often disowned by their families and the workhouse was the only place they could go during and after the birth of their child. Prior to the establishment of public mental asylums in the mid-nineteenth century (and in some cases even after that), the mentally ill and mentally handicapped poor were often consigned to the workhouse. Workhouses, though, were never prisons, and entry into them was generally a voluntary, although often painful, decision. It also carried with it a change in legal status—until 1918, receipt of poor relief meant a loss of the right to vote.

The operation of workhouses, and life and conditions inside them, varied over the centuries in the light of current legislation and economic and social conditions. The emphasis in earlier times was more towards the relief of destitution rather than deterrence of idleness which characterised many of the institutions set up under the 1834 Poor Law Amendment Act.[15]

Altogether 130 inmates, 86 males and 44 females, were recorded as being in the Union Workhouse at Chipping Norton in the 1901 census. The William Moss who died in 1903 and was buried in Ascott-under-Wychwood was probably Martha's husband.

BIOGRAPHIES

MARY MOSS (née Edginton) 1838–1908

OXFORD PRISON CHARGE SHEET RECORD MAY 1873

Name: Mary Moss; Married; Age 35. **Born:** [1838] Ascott-under-Wychwood.
Residence: Ascott-under-Wychwood. **Occupation:** gloveress.
Religion: Baptist. **Sentence:** 7 days with hard labour.

Mary Moss was named on the original wooden seat and on the charge sheet. Mary was related to six of the other women. She was sister-in-law to Caroline Moss, cousin by marriage to Jane, Charlotte, Amelia and Ann Moss, and cousin by marriage once removed to Mary Moss (Smith).

Mary was the fifth child and only daughter of Jonathan Edginton and his wife Ann, baptised on 26 August 1838 in Ascott-under-Wychwood. The year before she was born, Jonathan and Ann had lost two children, James (7) and Eli (5), who died in August 1837 within a week of each other. The cause of death is not known, but there were epidemics of measles and smallpox at that time.

In 1841, two-year-old Mary was living with her parents and three brothers: Jonathan (14), John (6), and six-month-old Stephen. Seven years later, in June 1848, Mary's brother Jonathan died at the age of 20.

In 1851, Mary (12) was living with her father, a woodman, her mother Ann, and her brother John (15), also a woodman, in Upper Street. Her brother Stephen (10) was staying with his uncle Caleb Edginton (29), in Church Street. Caleb worked as a farm labourer.

Mary married Alfred Moss, a carpenter and the brother of Caroline Moss, on 17 September 1859 in Ascott-under-Wychwood. In 1861 they were living with Mary's parents and her brother Stephen (20).

Mary and Alfred had no children of their own, but looked after their niece, Louise Ellen, Alfred's sister Ellen had died after giving birth to her in 1870. In 1871 Mary, Alfred, and 15-month-old Louise were living next door to Philip and Jane Pratley (probably the Jane Pratley who was not charged) and their one-year-old daughter Sarah.

In the 1881 census, 11-year-old Louise was still living with Mary (42), glove-maker, and Alfred (44), wheelwright.

In 1887 Alfred died, leaving Mary a widow with her niece Louise, then aged 17. Fourteen years later, in the 1901 census, Mary and 31-year-old

- 105 -

Louise, unmarried, were both living in Mill Lane and working as gloveresses. Mary Moss died in 1908, aged 70. She was buried in Ascott-under-Wychwood, where she had lived all her life.

ELIZABETH PRATLEY (née Osman) 1844–1873

OXFORD PRISON CHARGE SHEET RECORD MAY 1873
Name: Elizabeth Pratley; Married; Age 29. **Born**: [1844] Burford.
Residence: Ascott-under-Wychwood. **Occupation**: labourer [fieldworker].
Religion: Church of England. **Sentence**: 7 days with hard labour

Elizabeth Pratley's name was not on the original wooden seat, but it was on the charge sheet.

The charge sheet did not mention that Elizabeth had her nine-month-old baby, Eli, with her when she was sent to prison.

Elizabeth was related to seven of the other women. She was sister-in-law to Mary Pratley, aunt by marriage to Ellen Pratley, and niece by marriage to Amelia, Charlotte, and Ann Susan (Susannah) Moss, as well as to Levia Dring.

Elizabeth, baptised Ann Elizabeth on 26 May 1844 in Burford, was the first child born to William Osman and Maria Faulkner. Her sister Marianne, who was baptised on 1 November 1847, died the following year and was buried on 11 February 1848.

In 1851, seven-year-old Elizabeth was living at Wiggins Yard, Burford, with her parents, her one-year-old brother George, her three-month-old sister Emily, and her grandmother (67), a cook and pauper.

On 6 March 1869 in Burford, she married Eli Pratley from Ascott-under-Wychwood. He was the son of William Pratley, butcher and woodman, and Jemima Moss, Levia Dring's half-sister. Their first baby, also called Elizabeth, was born soon after, and baptised on 4 June 1869.

In 1871 Elizabeth and her daughter were staying in Mullinder's Charity, Burford, with her parents and her sisters, Ellen (11) and Fanny (7). Elizabeth's second baby, also named Ellen, was born in 1871 and baptised on 6 October 1872 in Ascott-under-Wychwood. On the same day her three-year-old sister Elizabeth was admitted to the church congregation. Their brother, two-month-old Eli, born on 16 August 1872 in Ascott-under-Wychwood, was baptised on 13 October 1872.

BIOGRAPHIES

Baby Eli was one of the two babies who went to prison with their mothers. Both he and his mother became unwell in prison, and Elizabeth was unable to attend the presentation function on the village green in June and receive her £5. Mary Pratley, her sister-in-law, may have accepted it on her behalf.

On 14 July 1873, seven weeks after leaving prison, Elizabeth, her husband, Eli, and their three children, Elizabeth (4), Ellen (2), and 11-month-old Eli, boarded the SS *Nyanza* in Plymouth for Canada. They reached Montreal in just over three weeks, on 5 August 1873, then moved to York, Toronto, where Elizabeth worked as a servant.

Elizabeth never recovered from the chill she caught on the way to gaol. She contracted a fever, probably while in the barracks, that was almost certainly typhus. This louse-borne infection commonly occurred in camps; also known as army-, camp-, famine-, ship-, or trench-fever, it was recognised as a 'barometer of human misery'.[16]

Elizabeth died on 26 September 1873, just six weeks after their arrival in Canada, from what was recorded as typhoid. Her widowed husband, Eli, and the children went back to Ascott, where his mother, Jemima, caught typhus from washing the family's soiled clothes. *Typhus rickettsia* can survive for several months on dirty clothes and is highly infectious if inhaled. Typhoid can only be passed to others through live bacteria, and is usually spread by human faeces or urine; the bacilli would die rapidly on contaminated clothing. It was not until early in the 20th century that microbiological tests provided a differential diagnosis, so the earlier confusion between these two infectious diseases was understandable. Jemima died in December 1873, followed in February 1874 by little Eli. For both, the cause of death was recorded as typhus.

Eli then found work as a groom on the Nightingale farm in Bishampton, near Pershore, in the neighbouring county of Worcestershire. He eloped with Jane Malins, a farm cook, and they married in Ascott in May 1874. In August 1874 Eli, Jane, and Eli's three-year-old daughter, Ellen, sailed to New Zealand on the *Crusader*. Eli's five-year-old daughter, also called Elizabeth, stayed in Burford with her grandparents, William and Maria Osman. In the 1901 census she was aged 30, a charwoman, living with her 79-year-old widowed grandfather, William Osman.

The emigrating family landed in Lyttelton, near Christchurch, 96 days later. They lived in the immigrants' barracks at Addington until Eli got work further south in Temuka. According to the 1903 *Cyclopaedia of New Zealand*:

> He went to Temuka, where he had to build his own house, as there were very few people in the district at that time. For about eight years he followed agriculture, and then, in conjunction with his brother and Mr Ward, he leased a farm of 128 acres near Temuka. After working this farm for three years he was burnt out of house and home by a destructive fire. The partnership was then dissolved and Mr Prattley took up another farm near at hand. There he worked for about five years, and built another house on a section he bought on the Arowhenua settlement. He then leased another farm from Mr Andrew Grant, and occupied it for four years. In 1895, he leased his present farm at Milford and now enjoys the results of persistent effort ...[17]

Not only had Eli become a farmer, he had become a landowner as well. Although he never attained the prosperity of his earlier counterparts 'back home' in England, he enjoyed the freedom of being his own boss.

Over time, Eli and Jane had eleven boys and one girl, as well as Eli's daughter, Ellen, ensuring that New Zealand was well populated with Pratley families. At some point Eli and Jane added an extra "t" to their surname, which enabled Fred's and Eli's families to be distinguished more easily.

Ellen, Elizabeth's younger daughter, did not have an easy life. Her stepmother Jane found her difficult, and Ellen was often sent elsewhere to live. She later married and had children. So, through Ellen, Eli's first wife, Elizabeth, has descendants living in New Zealand.

ELLEN PRATLEY (née Shayler) 1847–1921

OXFORD PRISON CHARGE SHEET RECORD MAY 1873
Name: Ellen Pratley; Married; Age 25. **Born:** [1847] Leafield.
Residence: Ascott-under-Wychwood. **Occupation:** gloveress.
Religion: Baptist. **Sentence:** 7 days with hard labour.

The original wooden seat named Ellen as Nelly Pratley. On the charge sheet her name was Ellen Pratley.

Ellen was related to six of the other women. She was the niece by marriage of Elizabeth and Mary Pratley, and great-niece by marriage to Levia Dring,

BIOGRAPHIES

Amelia Moss, and Ann Susan (Susannah) Moss. She was also first cousin once removed to Charlotte Moss.

Ellen was the third of eleven children born to George Shayler and Rosetta Hadland, both from Leafield. She was baptised in Leafield on 7 November 1847. At the time of her birth, her sister Mary-Ann was five years old and her brother Mark, two. In 1850, three years after Ellen was born, Charles arrived, followed by Luke in 1852, Philip in 1856, Hannah in 1859, Caroline in 1861, Jane in 1863, Jesse in 1865, and David in 1867. Jesse died when he was nine months old.

In the 1861 census Ellen (13) was still attending school. Her father was a woodman, her mother and Mary-Ann (19) were gloveresses, and Mark (16) was a carter. Charles (11), Luke (9), and Philip (5) were schoolboys, and Hannah (2) and two-month-old Caroline were at home. They were all living in Lower End, Leafield.

Ellen married John Pratley,[18] an agricultural labourer, on 30 October 1869 in Leafield. At the time of the 1871 census, Ellen and her husband (known as Jack or Jacky) were recorded as living in Church Yard Row, Charlbury, together with their one-year-old son, John. They were living next door to Ellen's brother, Charles Shayler, and his wife, Eleanor.

In 1871 Ellen's parents were living in Rangers Lodge, Leafield, with Luke (19), an agricultural labourer, and four other children; Philip (15), Hannah (13), Caroline (11) and Jane (8), all attending school. Ellen's father was a gamekeeper and her mother, a glovemaker.

In January 1872, Ellen and John's daughter Caroline was born, but died in April aged three months. Ellen's mother, Rosetta, died later the same year.

Some nine months after Ellen's imprisonment, in February 1874, she gave birth to twins; a boy, George, and a girl who did not survive. A year later, in 1875, Charles was born, followed by Philip in 1877 and Frank in 1879.

By 1881 Ellen, a glove-stitcher, and John, a labourer, were living in Ascott-under-Wychwood with their family of boys: John (11), George (7), Charles (5), Philip (4), and one-year-old Frank. All the older boys attended school. That year Philip died, and was buried on 19 August.

Two months later, on Friday 14 October, John drowned in the Evenlode River and was buried on 17 October. According to the *Oxford Times*, there had been a very strong gale. A number of trees had been blown down and

- 109 -

others damaged. During the gale, young John Pratley and Francis Longshaw were called to take a team of horses and a cartload of manure from William Lardner's homestead across a wooden bridge and into one of the fields on the other side of the Evenlode River. Before they reached the bridge, Francis was called away to help with one of the ricks where the thatch was being blown off by the wind.

John continued on, but while he was opening the gate to cross over the river, the wind 'took the gate with such force as to overpower him, and he was thrown into the river.'[19] When Francis returned, he found the team of horses with the cart had passed the field in which the manure should have been delivered, and were standing in a field beyond. There was no sign of John. John's father found his son's body in the water about two hours later, some 18 yards downstream of the bridge.[20]

The following year, 1882, Ellen gave birth to a girl, named Ellen. Albert was born three years later in 1885, followed by Lily in 1886, and Ernest in 1888. Rose, born in 1891, died when she was just three months old.

In the 1891 census, Ellen and John (Jack) were recorded as living in Mill Lane, Ascott-under-Wychwood, together with George (17), Charles (15), Frank (12), Albert (6), Ellen (9), Lily (4), and Ernest (2). John, George, Charles, and Frank were all agricultural labourers. Ernest died in 1895, aged seven, and was buried on 25 March.

When the 1901 census was taken, Ellen and John (Jack) were still in Mill Lane. John was recorded as a shepherd, Charlie (25) was a railway navvy, Frank (21) was an agricultural labourer, Albert (16) was a teamster, and Lily (14) was at home.

Ellen's daughter, Ellen, aged 19, had left her home in Ascott and was working as a housemaid in a boarding house in Eastbourne, Sussex. Also from Ascott, and working as a cook in the same boarding house, was Emma Beauchamp, granddaughter of Martha Smith (an Ascott martyr). Ellen's father, George Shayler, was a pauper living in the Chipping Norton Union Workhouse, where he died the following year. Ellen's youngest daughter, Lily, died in 1905, aged 18.

Ellen's husband, John, died in 1935, aged 86. He must have been a bit of a character, according to Doris Warner:

> I used to hear such tales from Old Age Pensioners too of the old days, especially from one old man, Jacky Pratley, a retired shepherd well over eighty. He could remember when

BIOGRAPHIES

the forest was cut down when it grew nearly to the Charlbury Road ... If you told him the date and time of the change of the moon, he would give you a weather forecast more accurate than the BBC. He would say, 'Ah my wench, I be the King of Ascott-under-Wychwood, and her up at the top thinks as her's the Queen' — 'her' being Mrs Chaundy of Yew Tree Farm who was on most committees ...[21]

Perhaps he expected to be 'King' of the household as well as the village, where he controlled his wife and family one way or another.

Ellen died in 1921 in Chipping Norton, aged 73.

Only five of Ellen and John's twelve children survived to adulthood. Their daughter Ellen was one of them. She died at the age of 80. The other four were George, who lived until he was 84; Charles, who reached 91; Frank, who reached 79; and Albert, who died at 75.

MARY PRATLEY (née Panting) 1839–1888

OXFORD PRISON CHARGE SHEET RECORD MAY 1873
Name: Mary Pratley; Married; Age 33. **Born:** [1839] Hailey.
Residence: Ascott-under-Wychwood. **Occupation:** labourer [field worker].
Religion: Methodist. **Sentence:** 7 days with hard labour.

Mary Pratley's name was on the original wooden seat and also on the charge sheet, which made no mention of the fact that Mary had her ten-week-old baby, Thomas, with her when she was sent to prison.

Mary was related by marriage to six of the other women. She was Elizabeth Pratley's sister-in-law, Ellen Pratley's aunt by marriage, and niece by marriage to Levia Dring, Amelia Moss, Charlotte Moss, and Ann Susan (Susannah) Moss.

Mary was born in the hamlet of Hailey on the southeastern edge of the old Wychwood Forest in West Oxfordshire. Her father, John Panting, was also born in Hailey; her mother, Mary Hanks, was born in Bampton about six miles southwest of Hailey. About five miles southeast of Ascott-under-Wychwood, Hailey is regarded as one of the Wychwood villages. It is only about a mile away from Ramsden, where the two youths, John Millin and John Hodgkins, lived.

When Mary was born, her sister Emma was four and her brother Thomas, two. Mary was baptised on 26 May 1839 in the old parish church in Hailey, which was built in 1761 and extended in 1830. In 1841, two-year-old Mary was living at Delley End, Hailey, with her father, John (33), an agricultural labourer; her mother, Mary, (38); her sister Emma (6); and four-year-old brother Thomas.

Ten years later, in the 1851 census, Mary (12) was living with her family at Ploughly End in Hailey. Her father and her brother Thomas (14), were farm labourers, and her three younger brothers were John (9), Richard (5) and one-year-old James. Her sister Emma was not at home.

Eight years later, in 1859, Mary's sister Emma married George Moss from Ascott-under-Wychwood. George's mother Esther Westbury came from Ramsden. His sister, Jane Moss, married John Pratley, Eli and Frederick's half-brother.

In 1861 Mary was 22 and living with her parents, John (53) and Mary (58), her brother Thomas (24) and his wife Elizabeth (24), and her brothers, John (17), Richard (14) and James (12), in rooms over stables on or near Merryfield Farm, Hailey. Her father was a farmer's carter, and all her brothers were agricultural labourers. Both Mary and her sister-in-law, Thomas's wife, Elizabeth, were recorded as agricultural labourers' servants.

Mary's sister Emma returned home to Hailey to have her firstborn, George Ernest, adding to the family of eight living in the rooms above the stables. Emma and baby George Ernest returned to Ascott-under-Wychwood for his baptism on 23 June 1861.

In 1861 Mary's husband-to-be, Frederick Pratley (19), worked as an agricultural labourer and lived at home in Ascott-under-Wychwood with his father, William, mother Jemima (née Moss), brothers William, Eli, Philip, and Charles, and sister Sarah Lucy (known as Lucy).

Two years later in 1863, at the age of 23, Mary gave birth to a boy, George Frederick Pratley Panting. After his birth she married Frederick Pratley (21) an agricultural labourer, on 10 October 1863 in Hailey. They moved some five miles away to Ascott-under-Wychwood where Frederick's parents, William and Jemima, lived. Also in the same year, Mary's sister Emma had a girl, Clara Esther Moss, who was baptised on 24 May 1863. For five years Mary lived close to her sister.

Mary and Frederick had five more children: Frederick James (1864), John William (1866), Charles Ernest (1868), Mary Ann (1870), and Thomas, (1873).

BIOGRAPHIES

In 1864, when Mary's second son was born, her sister Emma's three-year-old son, George Ernest Moss, died. Four years later her brother-in-law George died, in February 1868. He did not get to see his second daughter, Mary Ann, who was born later that same year.

Later in 1868, Mary and Emma's brother Richard married Eli and Frederick Pratley's sister, Sarah Lucy (known as Lucy).

In 1871 Mary's parents were living at White Oak Green in Hailey. Her father, John, was an agricultural labourer and shepherd. Her brother John, an agricultural labourer and carter, was unmarried and lived at home with his parents. Also in the household was Mary's widowed sister, Emma, and her two children, Clara (8) and Mary Ann (3). Emma was a gloveress. One of Mary's brothers, James, a carter, was married to Emma Millin, a gloveress from Ramsden. She was John Millin's[22] sister. Mary's father John died and was buried on 5 October 1871.

In 1873 Mary and Frederick with their family of six children were all living next door to Frederick's brother Eli, his wife, Elizabeth, and their three children in Ascott-under-Wychwood. There was also another family of six who lived in the same dwelling, an old workhouse built in the sixteenth century during the reign of Queen Elizabeth I.

A year after the women's imprisonment, Mary and Fredrick Pratley and their family were among the group who sailed for New Zealand on the clipper ship *Crusader* in September 1874. Mary was seven months pregnant and on the voyage gave birth to a baby girl who did not survive. The family arrived in New Zealand on 31 December 1874 and settled in Temuka, South Canterbury.

Seven months later, in July 1875, tragedy struck. Mary and Frederick were living in their farm house in Temuka, and one morning Mary made a short visit to her neighbour nearby. As Mary's young daughter, Mary Ann, was not well, she was left sitting on the hob near the fireplace to keep warm. When her mother returned to the house about ten minutes later she found the room full of smoke, and her daughter lying on the floor about three feet from the fire, with fatal burns.

In May 1877, Mary gave birth to another daughter, whom she also named Mary Ann. Another son, Arthur Henry, was born in September 1880. During that time the family leased a farm from a Mr Hayhurst, and remained there for twelve years. In 1888 Frederick Pratley took up a farm near Temuka.[23]

Mary contracted pneumonia in April 1888 and died six weeks later aged 48. Frederick Pratley later married Elizabeth Simmons from Lyneham, another Oxfordshire woman who had migrated to New Zealand, and had four more children.

MARTHA SMITH (née Hart) 1828– ?

OXFORD PRISON CHARGE SHEET RECORD MAY 1873
Name: Martha Smith; Married; Age 45. **Born:** [1828] Shilton.
Residence: Ascott-under-Wychwood. **Occupation:** labourer [field worker].
Religion: Church of England. **Sentence:** 10 days with hard labour.

Martha Smith's name was on the original wooden seat and also on the charge sheet. As she was considered one of the ringleaders, she was sentenced to ten days with hard labour. Martha was related to four of the other women. She was sister-in-law to Rebecca Smith, cousin (by marriage) once removed to Mary Moss (Smith), and cousin (by marriage) to Jane Moss and Fanny Honeybone.

Martha, the eldest child of George Hart and Leah Farmer, was baptised Martha Maria on 27 July 1828 in Shilton, in the neighbouring county of Berkshire.

In 1841 Martha (12), was living with her parents, her three brothers Alfred (10), John George (8), James (5), and her baby sister, Sarah Ellen. By 1851 Martha, now 22, had left home and was working as a general servant for Joseph Simmons, a farmer of 300 acres, in Long Combe, a parish in the Woodstock district of Oxfordshire. Joseph and his wife, Emma, had five children, their ages ranging from eight months to eight years. Joseph's mother also lived with them. Martha had two more sisters at home, Susannah (7) and Eliza (4). A year after the census, another sister, Fanny, arrived.

Martha married George Smith, son of Peter Smith and Mary Newman of Ascott-under-Wychwood, on 10 November 1856 in Asthally, Berkshire. George's grandfather, John Smith, had been married twice and had a total of eighteen children, ten with his first wife Rebecca Wilkins, and eight with his second wife, Maria Honnibone (*sic*). George's father Peter was the second to youngest in the second of John's families. In 1861 Martha and George were living with their two young daughters, Ellen Jane (3) and Eliza Emma (1), in Ascott-under-Wychwood.

Three more daughters had been added to the family by the time the 1871 census was taken: Rachel (9), Jane Maria (7), and Elizabeth Leah (4). Another daughter, Louisa, was born and baptised on 26 December 1869. She died when just over a year old and was buried on 17 January 1871. Two daughters were working for local tenant farmers: Ellen Jane (13) was a domestic servant for William Lardner at Manor Farm, and Eliza Emma (12) was working for Robert Hambidge at Crown Farm.

In 1880 a threshing machine arrived in Ascott-under-Wychwood and Martha's husband George, together with William Honeybone, was the first in the district to drive it. Tragically, while he was working on it, George's smock got caught in the machinery and he was drawn into the engine and killed. The vicar wrote in the parish magazine:

> on 19 February a fatal accident happened to George Smith (aged 50) employed on Mr Chaundy's farm, he was alone with a cutting machine, when it seems to have caught him by his smock and dragging him in to have strangled him causing him instant death. He leaves a widow and five children. He worked for Mr Chaundy for 25 years and proved himself to be a valuable and faithful servant.[24]

George Smith was buried on 23 February 1880 in Ascott-under-Wychwood.

In the 1881 census, Martha, a widow, was living next door to her daughter Ellen, her son-in-law Robert Beauchamp, and their two children, George (3) and six-month-old Emma. In the next cottage was Mary Pratley (née Mary Moss, otherwise Smith) with her husband George Pratley from Leafield, together with their four children. Martha's other four daughters, Rachel, Jane, Eliza, and Elizabeth, all worked as domestic servants in various households. Rachel (19) was a general domestic servant for Alfred and Mary Groves at 'The Elms' in nearby Milton-under-Wychwood. Alfred was a builder and employed forty men. Jane (17) was a servant in the Crown Inn, Shipton-under-Wychwood, where Ann Coombes was the innkeeper. Eliza (21) worked at Sandstone Castle, Iver, Buckingham, as a domestic servant for Frederick Garrard, an oil and seed broker. The youngest daughter, Elizabeth (15), worked for Robert Hambidge, as had her sister Eliza at an earlier period.

In the 1891 census, Martha was a charwoman and head of the household, now living with her eldest daughter, Ellen, her son-in-law Robert

Beauchamp, and three grandchildren. Robert was a cowman, young George (13) was a gardener's boy, while Emma (10) and Rachel (9) went to school. Martha cannot be found in the 1901 Census. She was not living with any of her daughters, and it is not known when or where she died.

MARY MOSS (otherwise Smith, later Mary Pratley) 1857–1890

OXFORD PRISON CHARGE SHEET RECORD MAY 1873
Name: Mary Moss, otherwise Smith; Single; Age 17. **Born:** [1857] Ascott-under-Wychwood. **Residence:** Ascott-under-Wychwood.
Occupation: Servant. **Religion:** Baptist. **Sentence:** 10 days with hard labour.

The name of Mary Moss was not on the original wooden seat, but on the charge sheet she was named as 'Mary Moss, otherwise Smith'.

Mary was related to six of the other women. She was niece to Jane Moss, and a cousin (by marriage) once removed to Mary Moss, Caroline Moss, Charlotte Moss, Amelia Moss, and Ann Moss.

Mary was born to a single woman, Eliza Smith, and baptised on 4 January 1857 in Ascott-under-Wychwood. Five years later, on 4 April 1863 in Ascott, Eliza married Thomas Moss, son of Thomas Moss and Ann Wiggins and grandson of William Moss and Susannah Scarsebrook.

Two years after Mary was imprisoned with the other women, she married George Pratley, son of Edward Pratley and Caroline Acres of Leafield, on 20 September 1875. As already noted, Pratley was a common surname in the area, but there were quite distinct ancestral lines. Although George shared the same surname as Eli and Frederick Pratley, they were not obviously related.

Six years later, in the 1881 census, Mary and George, an agricultural labourer, were living in Ascott-under-Wychwood together with their four children: George Thomas (5) and Charles (4), both schoolboys, Mary (2), and seven-month-old Fanny. Over the following nine years, Mary and George had five more children: Henry (1883), Walter (1884) Alfred (1886), Maria (1888), and Edward (1890). Both Mary and baby Edward survived only a few days after his birth. Edward was baptised on 11 February 1890, and buried, together with his mother, on 17 February 1890. She was 33 years old.

BIOGRAPHIES

For the next six years, George continued to manage alone, probably with help from Mary's extended family in the village. In the 1891 census, a widower aged 35, he was employed as a gardener and living with his eight surviving children: Thomas (15), Charles (14), Mary (12), Fanny (10), Henry (8), Walter (6), Alfred (5), and Maria (2). Thomas and Charles both worked as plough boys. Mary, Fanny, Henry, Walter, and Alfred all went to school.

George Pratley married Emma Rhyman on 23 May 1896, in Middleton Stoney, Oxfordshire, and they went on to have four children: Reginald, Gwendoline, William, and Rosa. In 1901, George and Emma were living in Church Street, Buckden, Huntingdonshire, with the youngest two children from George's first marriage to Mary, and the first three of their own. George was a gardener and his son Alfred (14) a farm labourer.

As they grew to adulthood, the children from George's first marriage to Mary moved away from Ascott-under-Wychwood. George Thomas (later known as Thomas) married Ethel Emmett on 1 June 1903, in High Wycombe, Buckinghamshire. They had six children. George died in Pontypridd, Wales.

In 1898 Charles married Margaret Lewis, from Pontypridd. In 1901 they were living at 32 Wingfield Crescent, Llanfabon, Glamorganshire, Wales. Charles was a haulier in a coalmine. They had a total of five children.

By 1901 daughter Mary was married to Charles Hilton, a painter's labourer, and living at 14 Lower Road, Eastbourne, East Sussex. They had two young sons, Charles (3) and William (1).

Fanny had a son, Charles Henry Pratley, in 1897. She married a Mr Metters in 1900 in Pontypridd. In the 1901 census, Henry, aged 18 and single, was a coal miner, and an inmate in the Union Workhouse in Chipping Norton. Walter married a Miss Whitney in Pontypridd in 1904, and they had four children. Maria married a Mr Adams in Pontypridd in 1906, but she died the same year.

The history of Pontypridd is closely tied to the coal and iron industries. Prior to these being developed, Pontypridd was largely a rural backwater comprising a few farmsteads, with Treforest initially becoming the main urban settlement in the area. Sited at the junction of the three valleys, it became central to the transportation of coal from the Rhondda and iron from Merthyr Tydfil, first via the Glamorganshire Canal and later via the Taff Vale Railway, to the ports at Cardiff and Barry and to Newport. Because of its role in transporting coal cargo, Pontypridd's railway platform was once thought to have been the longest in the world. By the second half of the nineteenth century Pontypridd was a hive of industry and nicknamed the 'Wild West'.[25]

REBECCA SMITH (née Belcher) 1846–1920

OXFORD PRISON CHARGE SHEET RECORD MAY 1873
Name: Rebecca Smith; Married: [Charles Smith]; Age 25 [actually 27].
Born: [1846] Churchill. **Residence**: Ascott-under-Wychwood.
Occupation: labourer [field worker]. **Religion**: Church of England.
Sentence: 10 days with hard labour.

Rebecca Smith's name was on the original seat as Becky Smith. Her name on the charge sheet was Rebecca Smith.

Rebecca was related to four of the other women. She was sister-in-law to Martha Smith, cousin (by marriage) once removed to Mary Moss (Smith), and cousin (by marriage) to Jane Moss and Fanny Honeybone.

The daughter of Charles Belcher and Elizabeth Betteridge of Kingham, a village about four miles southwest of Chipping Norton, Rebecca was baptised on 20 September 1846, in the village of Churchill, about a mile away. Both villages are about four miles northwest of Ascott-under-Wychwood. In 1851 she was living with her parents and sister, two-year-old Sarah, in Kingham.

Ten years later, in 1861, Rebecca (14) was living at home with her parents and five siblings. Her two brothers were Joseph (9) and Alan (6). Her three sisters were Sarah (12), Elizabeth (4), and Phillis (1). Rebecca worked away from home as a servant.

In 1865, aged about seventeen, Rebecca gave birth to a daughter, Sarah. Two years later she married Martha Smith's half-brother, Charles Smith, on 16 November 1867. His mother, Mary Smith, had been a widow for two years when she gave birth to Charles, who was baptised on 27 May 1838. Three years later, when Charles was three years old, Mary married Thomas Tymms on 23 September 1841.

In the 1871 census, Rebecca and Charles were recorded under the surname of Tymms. They had three children: Sarah Ann Robbins Belcher (5), George (3), and one-year-old Thomas. Later records of the family showed their surname once again to be Smith. They lived in a cottage facing Coldstone Farm on the double bend at the west end of Ascott-under-Wychwood.[26]

Back in Kingham, in the 1871 census, Rebecca's mother, Elizabeth, was the head of the household, living with her daughters Phillis (11) and Mary Ann (8), who both went to school. Rebecca's father, Charles, was lodging with Jeremiah and Mary Hooper and their sons Walter (12) and Albert (2) at Square Ditch Pike in Shipton Solars, Gloucestershire. Both Charles and Jeremiah were employed as road labourers, and Jeremiah's wife, Mary, was a toll-gate keeper.

In the 1881 census, Rebecca was working as a gloveress, but her husband Charles continued to work as an agricultural labourer. Living with them were five of their six children. Their eldest son George (13) was a ploughboy. Thomas (11), Phillis (7), and Louisa (5) attended school. Their youngest child, Elizabeth, was aged two.

Rebecca Smith.
(Peoples History Museum, Manchester, UK.)

Rebecca's eldest child Sarah (15) was employed as a domestic servant to Frederick Parsons, a general draper, who lived in Chipping Norton with his wife, Susannah, and children Winifred (5), Ethel (3), and one-year-old Charles. Also in the household were Frederick's nephew, Harry Vorley, a cabinet maker, and another domestic servant, Eleanor Collins.

In the 1891 census, Rebecca and Charles's son Thomas was working as an agricultural labourer, while Elizabeth (12) and two more sons, Charles (5) and Fred (3) went to school.

By the 1901 census, Rebecca and Charles were still living in the original cottage with their two youngest sons, Charles (15) and Fred (13), who worked as teamsters. A grandson, eight-year-old Wallace, also lived with them.

Rebecca died in 1920, aged 74. Charles Smith died in December 1918, aged 80.

THE OTHER FOUR WOMEN named on the original seat

Brief notes on the lives of the four women, Celia Honeybone, Elizabeth Honeybone, Eliza Honeybone, Jane Pratley, whose names were inscribed on the original eight-sided wooden seat, but were not on the charge list, are given below.

Celia and Elizabeth Honeybone

Celia Honeybone would have been six years old in 1873; her sister Elizabeth was sixteen. Their father was one of two William Honeybones. One was the illegitimate son of Mary Honeybone, baptised on 27 February 1814; he married Caroline (née Tymms). There is no record for the other William showing who his parents were, but from the census records it can be estimated that he was born in 1818. He married Eleanor Moss (Doris Warner's grandmother), who became the mother of Celia and Elizabeth.

Eliza Honeybone (Sirman)

In 1873 Eliza Honeybone was 36 years old and married to John Sirman. They had six children between the ages of two and thirteen. In 1871 they were living in Crawley, two and a half miles north of Witney, and in 1875 they were in Enstone, about four miles east of Chipping Norton. Eliza was the daughter of John and Jane Honeybone, and sister to Jane Moss and Fanny Honeybone, who were both imprisoned. Their father was the illegitimate son of Sarah Honeybone.

The three older Honeybone couples and their families, William and Caroline, William and Eleanor, and John and Jane, were all living in Ascott-under-Wychwood at the same time. Two of these families had eleven children each, the other had nine children. Working out who belonged to which family could be confusing. Even the Honeybones, Smiths, and Mosses themselves, and more latterly the Pratleys, could be forgiven for not knowing who were related and who were not.

Jane Pratley

Jane was summonsed but not found guilty. She was probably the daughter of Joseph Pratley and Esther Holloway, and the wife of Philip Pratley, son of John and Jane Pratley. Again, although Philip and Jane shared the same surname before they married, they were not related closely, if at all. In 1873 Jane was 31 years old and had two small children, Sarah (3) and one-year-old Fanny, with another child due in three months' time.

Philip and Jane, with their three children, were the first of the Pratleys to emigrate to New Zealand, leaving England on the *Mongol* on 23 December 1873. Unfortunately measles and scarlet fever had been brought on board, and there were over fifty cases reported in the first four weeks.[27] By the time the ship reached New Zealand, fifteen children had died[28] including Philip and Jane's second daughter, 20-month-old Fanny.

ENDNOTES

INTRODUCTION
1 Hodgkins, J. R. (1978), *Over the Hills to Glory: Radicalism in Banburyshire 1832–1945*, Clifton Press, Southend.
2 There were two charge sheets, officially known as warrants of commitment. The first listed nine of the women, and the second listed the other seven. They are held as items CPZ 16/1 and CPZ 16/2 in the Oxfordshire Archives, Oxford County Records Office, Oxford.

CHAPTER 1
1 'Statement of the Ascott Farmers', *Oxfordshire Weekly News*, 4 June 1873.
2 *Oxford Chronicle and Berks & Bucks Gazette*, 31 May 1873.
3 Ottewell, Gordon (2004), *The Evenlode: An Exploration of a Cotswold River*, Green Branch Press, Gloucester.
4 Oxfordshire Federation of Women's Institutes (1999), *The Oxfordshire Village Book*, Countryside Books, Newbury Berkshire.
5 Ottewell, Gordon (2004).
6 From Ascott Archives, 1997.
7 Montgomery-Massingberd, Hugh (2004), *Blenheim and the Churchills*, Jarrold Publishing, UK.
8 Mann, Ralph (1997), interviewed by Jock Phillips, Chief Historian, New Zealand Department of Internal Affairs, in Ascott-under-Wychwood, April.
9 Jourdan, Sue, and Rawlins, John (1990), *The Second Wychwoods Album*, Wychwoods Local History Society, Shipton-under-Wychwood.
10 http://en.wikipedia.org/wiki/Ascott-under-Wychwood.
11 By 1875, John Hill, a carpenter, was the licensee. One of his sons, John, was a baker, and his other son, George, was a maltster, who brewed the beer.
12 Warner, Doris (1999), *My Personal Memories*, Wychwood Press, Charlbury.

ENDNOTES

13 Honeybone, Harry (1933), 'Part of the Life History of Harry Honeybone', Unpublished manuscript, held by B. McCombs, Wellington, New Zealand.
14 Honeybone, Harry (1933).
15 William and his first wife Lucy had another son, Philip, but he died in 1843, aged 11.
16 Jourdan, Sue and Richards, Sue (1985), *The Wychwoods Album*, Wychwoods Local History Society, Shipton-under-Wychwood.
17 Moss, Eric (1999), *Walk Humble, My Son*, Wychwood Press, Charlbury.
18 Honeybone, Harry (1933).
19 *Oxfordshire Weekly News*, 4 June 1873.
20 Samuel, Raphael (ed.) (1975), *Village Life and Labour*, Routledge & Kegan Paul, London and Boston, p. 127.
21 Kitteringham, Jennie, (1975), 'Part 3: Country work girls in ninteenth-century England' p. 128, in History Workshop Series *Village Life and Labour*, edited by R. Samuel. Routledge & Kegan Paul, London and Boston.
22 Horn, Pamela (ed.) (1974), *Agricultural Trade Unionism in Oxfordshire 1872-81*, Oxfordshire Record Society, Vol. XLVIII, Oxford.
23 *The Times*, 14 June 1873.
24 *Oxfordshire Weekly News*, 2 July 1873.
25 *The Times*, 14 June, 1873.
26 *Oxfordshire Weekly News*, 2 July 1873.
27 *The Times*, 14 June 1873.
28 *Oxfordshire Weekly News*, 2 July 1873.

CHAPTER 2

1 Woodstock is about 10 miles from Ascott-under-Wychwood and Charlbury is about 3 miles away.
2 Leyland, N. L. and Troughton, J. E. (1974), 'Glovemaking in West Oxfordshire', Oxford City and County Museum Publication No 4, Oxford.
3 Horn, Pamela (c.1998), 'Gloving by hand—a dying craft', *Limited Edition Magazine (Herts & Bucks)*, Buckinghamshire.
4 Warner, Doris (1999).
5 Horn, Pamela (c.1998).
6 Arnold, Rollo (1981), *The Farthest Promised Land: English Villagers, New Zealand Immigrants of the 1870s*, Victoria University Press with Price Milburn, Wellington, NZ, p. 113.
7 Arnold, Rollo (1981), p. 113.
8 Mingay, G. E. (1998), *Rural Life in Victorian England*, Alan Sutton Publishing Ltd., Gloucester, p. 117.

9   Warner, Doris (1999).
10 Miller, Celia (ed.) (1983), *Rain and Ruin: the Diary of an Oxfordshire Farmer, John Simpson Calvertt 1875-1900*, Alan Sutton Publishing Ltd, Gloucester.
11 Honeybone, Harry (1933).
12 Honeybone, Harry (1933).
13 Honeybone, Harry (1933).
14 Mingay, G. E. (1998), p. 75.
15 Hardy, Thomas (1883), 'The Dorsetshire Labourer', reprinted in Golby, J. M. (ed.) (1986), *Culture and Society in Britain, 1850-1890: A Source Book of Contemporary Writings*, Oxford University Press, Oxford, p.303.
16 Mingay, G. E. (1998).
17 Mingay, G. E. (1998), p. 304.
18 http://en.wikipedia.org/wiki/Hay
19 Mingay, G. E. (1998), p. 81.
20 Hardy, Thomas (1883), p. 304.
21 Kitteringham, Jennie (1975), p. 128.
22 Kitteringham, Jennie (1975).
23 Between 1 April 1871 and 20 March 1872 was the wettest year on record in England and Wales until 2001. *Evening Post*, 24 March 2001. The record has since been broken again, in 2014.
24 *Oxford Chronicle and Berks & Bucks Gazette*, 7 June 1873.
25 *Oxford Chronicle and Berks & Bucks Gazette*, 15 May 1858.
26 Horn, Pamela (1971), *Joseph Arch: The Farm Workers' Leader*, The Roundwood Press, Kineton.
27 *Oxford Chronicle and Berks & Bucks Gazette*, 5 May 1866.
28 Elizabeth was one of the sixteen women sent to prison. She took her baby, Eli, with her.
29 *Oxford Times*, 12 February 1870.

CHAPTER 3

1   *Oxfordshire Weekly News*, 4 June 1873.
2   *Oxfordshire Weekly News*, 4 June 1873.
3   Scarth, Bob (1998), *"We'll all be union men': the story of Joseph Arch and his Union men*, Industrial Pioneer Publications, Coventry.
4   *The Times*, 20 January 1873.
5   O'Leary, John Gerard (ed.) (1966), *The Autobiography of Joseph Arch*, MacGibbon & Kee, London.
6   Honeybone, Harry (1933).

ENDNOTES

7 John Henry Tymms was baptised on 15 July 1866. His parents were John and Caroline (née Newman) Tymms. On immigrating to New Zealand, the family later changed their surname to Timms.
8 Timms, J. H. (2002), 'A Story Reminiscent of my First Plum Pudding', in *The Clipper Ship Crusader 1865–1910: Memories and Records of Over Fifty Years' Pioneering*, Cadsonbury Publications, Christchurch, NZ.
9 Mann, Ralph (1982), interviewed by Robin Thompson and published in the *Witney Gazette*, 7 October 1982.
10 Horn, Pamela (ed.) (1974).
11 Taunt, Henry W. (c. 1910), 'Joseph Arch and the Labourer's Union', Pamphlet n.d. D97/1888, Centre for Oxfordshire Studies, Oxford.
12 Taunt, Henry W. (c. 1910).
13 Taunt, Henry W. (c. 1910).
14 Taunt, Henry W. (c. 1910).
15 Horn, Pamela (ed.) (1974) p. 26.
16 Horn, Pamela (ed.) (1974) p. 27.
17 Horn, Pamela (ed.) (1974), p. 31.
18 Arnold, Rollo (1981), p. 33.
19 Arnold, Rollo (1981), p. 33.
20 Arnold, Rollo (1981), p. 34.
21 Horn, Pamela (ed.) (1974), p. 27.
22 This is the first reference to Frederick S. Attenborough and his involvement with the union.
23 http://www.teara.govt.nz/en/history-of-immigration/8/6

CHAPTER 4

1 *Oxfordshire Weekly News*, 4 June 1873.
2 *Daily News*, 27 May 1873.
3 *Oxfordshire Weekly News*, 4 June 1873.
4 *Oxfordshire Weekly News*, 4 June 1873.
5 *Oxfordshire Weekly News*, 4 June 1873.
6 *Oxford Chronicle and Berks & Bucks Gazette*, 7 June 1873.
7 Another farmer, John Calvertt, wrote in his diary in 1877 that the fox hunts regularly killed 122 foxes in 121 days.
8 *Daily News*, 27 May 1873.
9 *Oxfordshire Weekly News*, 4 June 1873.
10 *Oxfordshire Weekly News*, 4 June 1873.
11 *Oxford Chronicle and Berks & Bucks Gazette*, 7 June 1873.

12 *Oxfordshire Weekly News*, 4 June 1873.
13 *Oxfordshire Weekly News*, 4 June 1873.
14 *Oxfordshire Weekly News*, 4 June 1873.

CHAPTER 5

1 Warrant of commitment CPZ 16/1, Oxfordshire Archives, Oxford.
2 Ellen was the wife of John Pratley, son of Eli and Frederick's half-brother.
3 Warrant of commitment CPZ 16/1, Oxfordshire Archives, Oxford.
4 Jane was probably the wife of Philip Pratley, son of Eli and Frederick's half-brother.
5 Warner, Doris (1953), *Over the Hills to Glory*, play registered at Stationers' Hall, London.
6 1871 Census, Census Returns of England and Wales, The National Archives, Kew, Surrey.
7 *Jackson's Oxford Journal*, 24 May 1873. The journal was a regional newspaper published between 1753 and 1926.
8 *Oxfordshire Weekly News*, 28 May 1873.
9 In fact, Robert Hambidge was away at the Stow Fair that day.
10 *Oxfordshire Weekly News*, 28 May 1873.
11 *Oxfordshire Weekly News*, 28 May 1873.
12 *Oxfordshire Weekly News*, 28 May 1873.
13 But Hodgkins said she was not round the gate.
14 *Oxfordshire Weekly News*, 28 May 1873.
15 *Oxfordshire Weekly News*, 28 May 1873.
16 *Oxfordshire Weekly News*, 28 May 1873.
17 In this quote, Martha Smith seems to have taken the stance that the strike was actually a lockout, but this was not the case.
18 *Oxfordshire Weekly News*, 4 June 1873.
19 *Oxfordshire Weekly News*, 4 June 1873.
20 Lady Clara Vere de Vere is a fictional aristocrat in a poem written by Alfred Tennyson. See his *Collected Poems*, published in 1842: http://en.wikipedia.org/wiki/Lady_Clara_Vere_de_Vere.
21 *Daily News* [n.d.],CPZ 16/35 Oxfordshire Archives.
22 *Oxfordshire Weekly News*, 4 June 1873.
23 *Oxfordshire Weekly News*, 4 June 1873.
24 *Daily News* [n.d.], CPZ 16/35 Oxfordshire Archives.
25 *Oxfordshire Weekly News*, 28 May 1873.
26 *Oxfordshire Weekly News*, 28 May 1873.

ENDNOTES

27 *Oxford Chronicle and Berks & Bucks Gazette*, 31 May 1873.
28 Warrant of commitment on a conviction where the punishment is by imprisonment under s. 24, CPZ 16/1, Oxfordshire Archives, Oxford.
29 *Oxfordshire Weekly News*, 4 June 1873.

CHAPTER 6

1 *Oxfordshire Weekly News*, 11 June 1873.
2 *Banbury Guardian*, 29 May 1873.
3 *Banbury Guardian*, 29 May 1873.
4 *Oxfordshire Weekly News*, 28 May 1873.
5 *Oxfordshire Weekly News*, 28 May 1873.
6 *Oxford Chronicle and Berks & Bucks Gazette*, 31 May 1873.
7 *Oxfordshire Weekly News*, 28 May 1873.
8 *Oxford Chronicle and Berks & Bucks Gazette*, 31 May 1873.
9 *Oxford Chronicle and Berks & Bucks Gazette*, 31 May 1873.
10 *Oxfordshire Weekly News*, 28 May 1873.
11 *Oxfordshire Weekly News*, 28 May 1873.
12 *Oxfordshire Weekly News*, 28 May 1873.
13 *Oxfordshire Weekly News*, 11 June 1873.
14 *Oxfordshire Weekly News*, 11 June 1873.
15 *Oxfordshire Weekly News*, 11 June 1873.
16 *Oxfordshire Weekly News*, 28 May 1873.
17 *Oxfordshire Weekly News*, 28 May 1873.
18 *Oxfordshire Weekly News*, 11 June 1873.
19 *Oxfordshire Weekly News*, 28 May 1873.
20 *Oxfordshire Weekly News*, 28 May 1873.
21 *Oxfordshire Weekly News*, 11 June 1873.
22 *The Times*, 26 May 1873.
23 *Oxford Chronicle and Berks & Bucks Gazette*, 31 May 1873.
24 *Oxford Chronicle and Berks & Bucks Gazette*, 24 May 1873.
25 *Oxford Chronicle and Berks & Bucks Gazette*, 24 May 1873.

CHAPTER 7

1 *Oxford Chronicle and Berks & Bucks Gazette*, 31 May 1873.
2 *Oxford Chronicle and Berks & Bucks Gazette*, 7 June 1873.
3 *Oxfordshire Weekly News*, 4 June 1873.
4 Author's personal conversation with a police constable in Chipping Norton.
5 Warrant of commitment on a conviction where the punishment is by

THE ASCOTT MARTYRS

imprisonment under s. 24, CPZ 16/1 Oxfordshire Archives.
6 Rules for the Government of the Prison of the County of Oxford called the Oxford Castle 1855.
7 Rules for the Government of the Prison of the County of Oxford called the Oxford Castle 1855.
8 Rules for the Government of the Prison of the County of Oxford called the Oxford Castle 1855.
9 *Oxford Chronicle and Berks & Bucks Gazette*, 7 June 1873.
10 Rules for the Government of the Prison of the County of Oxford called the Oxford Castle 1855.
11 *Oxford Chronicle and Berks & Bucks Gazette*, 7 June 1873.
12 *Oxford Chronicle and Berks & Bucks Gazette*, 7 June 1873.
13 *Oxford Chronicle and Berks & Bucks Gazette*, 7 June 1873.
14 *Oxfordshire Weekly News*, 28 May 1873.
15 *Oxfordshire Weekly News*, 28 May 1873.
16 Letter to the Lord Chancellor from the Duke of Marlborough, 18 June 1873.
17 Palmer, Edwin (1888), 'Appeal by the Archdeacon of Oxford for the Funds to Extend the Laundry', Pamphlet OXFO 365, Oxfordshire County Libraries.
18 The National Trust (2004), 'The Laundry' in *Mothballs and Elbow Grease*, National Trust (Enterprises) Ltd, Wiltshire.
19 The National Trust, (2004).
20 The National Trust, (2004).
21 The National Trust, (2004).
22 http://wokingprison.blogspot.co.nz/2009/02/prison-laundry.html.
23 http://wokingprison.blogspot.co.nz/2009/02/prison-laundry.html.
24 Visiting Justices report C2 16/11, Oxfordshire Archives, Oxford.
25 *Oxfordshire Weekly News*, 28 May 1873.

CHAPTER 8

1 Honeybone, Harry (1933).
2 Ascott School Log Book, 1863-1887, Ref. S/09/1/A1/1, Centre for Oxfordshire Studies, Oxford.
3 Timms, J.H., (1928).
4 *Oxford Chronicle and Berks & Bucks Gazette*, 31 May 1873.
5 *Oxford Chronicle and Berks & Bucks Gazette*, 31 May 1873.

ENDNOTES

CHAPTER 9
1 *Oxfordshire Weekly News*, 4 June 1873.
2 *Oxfordshire Weekly News*, 4 June 1873.
3 *Oxfordshire Weekly News*, 4 June 1873.
4 *Oxford Chronicle and Berks & Bucks Gazette*, 31 May 1873.
5 *Oxfordshire Weekly News*, 4 June 1873.
6 *Oxfordshire Weekly News*, 4 June 1873.
7 *Banbury Guardian*, 29 May 1873.
8 *Banbury Guardian*, 29 May 1873.
9 *Banbury Guardian*, 29 May 1873.
10 *Oxfordshire Weekly News*, 4 June 1873.
11 Gabriel George Banbury (1815-1911) was a prosperous draper of Woodstock, and had been a Methodist local preacher from 1835.
12 Ascott-under-Wychwood Church of England Primary School Log Book, 1863-1887.
13 Arnold, Rollo (1981), p. 124.
14 http://www.teara.govt.nz/en/history-of-immigration/8/6.
15 *Oxfordshire Weekly News*, 4 June 1873.
16 *Daily News*, 27 May 1873.
17 *Daily News*, 27 May 1873.
18 Mann, Ralph (c.1985), The Ascott Martyrs, unpublished notes.
19 Copy of the Post Office Telegraph, CPZ16/6, Oxfordshire Archives, Oxford.
20 Van der Kiste, John (1986), *Queen Victoria's Children*, Alan Sutton Publishing Ltd, Gloucester.
21 *Oxford Chronicle and Berks & Bucks Gazette*, 7 June 1873.
22 *Oxford Chronicle and Berks & Bucks Gazette*, 7 June 1873.
23 *Oxford Chronicle and Berks & Bucks Gazette*, 7 June 1873.
24 *Oxfordshire Weekly News*, 4 June 1873.
25 *Oxford Chronicle and Berks & Bucks Gazette*, 7 June 1873.
26 *Oxford Chronicle and Berks & Bucks Gazette*, 7 June 1873.
27 *Oxfordshire Weekly News*, 4 June, 1873.
28 *Oxford Chronicle and Berks & Bucks Gazette*, 7 June 1873.
29 *Oxford Chronicle and Berks & Bucks Gazette*, 7 June 1873.
30 *Oxford Chronicle and Berks & Bucks Gazette*, 7 June 1873.
31 *Oxford Chronicle and Berks & Bucks Gazette*, 7 June 1873.

CHAPTER 10

1. Chastleton is a village and civil parish in the Cotswold Hills in Oxfordshire, about 8 miles west of Swerford.
2. Slapton is a village and also a civil parish within Aylesbury Vale district in Buckinghamshire, England.
3. Miller, Celia (ed.) (1983).
4. John Charles was Calvertt's son.
5. Miller, Celia (ed.) 1983.
6. *Oxfordshire Weekly News*, 28 May 1873.
7. *Oxfordshire Weekly News*, 28 May 1873.

CHAPTER 11

1. *Daily News*, 27 May 1873. (CPZ 16/4, Oxfordshire Archives.)
2. *The Times*, 29 May 1873.
3. Sir William Blackstone, author of *The Commentaries on the Laws of England*.
4. *Daily News*, 27 May 1873.
5. *Daily News*, 27 May 1873.
6. *The Times*, 29 May 1873
7. *The Oxfordshire Weekly News*, 4 June 1873.
8. *The Oxfordshire Weekly News*, 4 June 1873.
9. Letter written by Lord Selborne to the Duke of Marlborough, 4 June 1873. CPZ 16/9, Oxfordshire Archives.
10. Letter written by Lord Selborne to the Duke of Marlborough, 4 June 1873. CPZ 16/9, Oxfordshire Archives.
11. Letter written by the Duke of Marlborough to the Lord Chancellor, Selborne, 18 June 1873. Personal collection of Ralph Mann.
12. *Oxfordshire Weekly News*, 11 June 1873.
13. *Oxfordshire Weekly News*, 11 June 1873.
14. *Oxford Chronicle and Berks & Bucks Gazette*, 7 June 1873.
15. *Jackson's Oxford Journal*, 14 June 1873.
16. *Oxfordshire Weekly News*, 25 June 1873.
17. *Oxfordshire Weekly News*, 25 June 1873.

CHAPTER 12

1. *The Times*, 3 June 1873.
2. *The Times*, 3 June, 1873, CPZ 16/8 Oxfordshire Archives.
3. Baby Eli was born on 16 August 1872, so was actually 9 months at the time.
4. *The Times*, 3 June 1873, CPZ 16/8 Oxfordshire Archives.

ENDNOTES

5 *Oxfordshire Weekly News*, 11 June 1873.
6 *Oxfordshire Weekly News*, 11 June 1873.
7 *The Times*, 3 July 1873.
8 *Oxford Chronicle and Berks & Bucks Gazette*, 31 May 1873.
9 *Oxford Chronicle and Berks & Bucks Gazette*, 31 May 1873
10 *Oxford Chronicle and Berks & Bucks Gazette*, 31 May 1873.
11 *Oxford Chronicle and Berks & Bucks Gazette*, 31 May 1873.
12 *Oxford Chronicle and Berks and Bucks Gazette*, 7 June, 1873.

CHAPTER 13

1 *Oxfordshire Weekly News*, 25 June, 1873.
2 *Oxfordshire Weekly News*, 25 June, 1873.
3 Tape recording: 'Lifting the Latch, the Life of Mont Abbott (1902-1989)', author's copy.
4 *Oxfordshire Weekly News*, 25 June 1873.
5 I have not located any copies of the quoted letters.
6 *Oxfordshire Weekly News*, 25 June 1873.
7 *Oxfordshire Weekly News*, 25 June 1873.

CHAPTER 14

1 Mann, Ralph (c.1985) The Ascott Martyrs, unpublished notes.
2 http://en.wikipedia.org/wiki/William_Ewart_Gladstone.
3 http://en.wikipedia.org/wiki/Reform_Act_1884.
4 Mann, Ralph (c.1985), The Ascott Martyrs, unpublished notes.
5 Green, Frederick Ernest (1920), *A History of the English Agricultural Labourer, 1870-1920*, P.S. King & Son, Westminster, London.
6 McQuay, Tom, and Waugh, Duncan (1996), 'A Determined Emigrant', *Wychwoods History, the Journal of the Wychwoods Local History Society*, Number Eleven, 1996.
7 See Elizabeth's biography for details of the confusion between these two diseases.

EPILOGUE

1 Timms, J.H. (1928).
2 Kibble, John (1999), *Charming Charlbury with its Nine Hamlets & Chipping Norton*, pp197–198, First published 1927. The Wychwood Press, Charlbury.
3 *Jackson's Oxford Journal*, 22 May 1873 and 28 June 1873.

4   Hodgkins, J. R. (1978), p. 66.
5   Meades, Eileen (1949), *History of Chipping Norton*, Poundstone Press England.
6   Groves, Reginald (1949),*Sharpen the Sickle!: The History of the Farm Workers' Union*, reprinted 2011 by Porcupine Press, Michigan, pp. 59-60.
7   Horn, Pamela (1971).
8   Walton, R. M. (1961) 'The Ascott Women', Top. Oxon. No. 6, Oxford.
9   Finn, Elizabeth (1987), 'The Ascott Women', unpublished essay lodged in the Oxfordshire Archives]
10 Personal letter from the Trades Union Congress, 14 August 1990, in response to a query from the author.
11 Arnold, Rollo (1981).
12 Arnold Rollo (1981), pp. 119-125.
13 Warner, Doris (1999).
14 The farmers said it was beans that needed hoeing.
15 The demonstration was reported as being in the marketplace, Chipping Norton.
16 'A Stirring Memory of Fifty-Five Years Ago', interview with Fanny Rathband, the youngest Ascott martyr, in *The Land Worker*, December 1928.
17 Moss, Eric R. (1999).
18 Moss, Eric R. (1999), p. 47.
19 Jock Phillips, personal communication, including copy of interview, April 1997.
20 Sandys, Elspeth (1996), *Riding to Jerusalem*, Hodder Moa Beckett, Auckland, NZ.
21 Sandys Elspeth (1996).
22 http://www.historic-uk.com/HistoryUK/England-History/AscotMartyrs. htm and http://www.webcitation.org/query?url=http://www.geocities.com/ Heartland/Plains/6081/&date=2009-10-25+07:46:50.

BIOGRAPHIES

1   This information came from an email to the author from a great granddaughter of Levia's.
2   Evening Post, Wellington, NZ, 26 March 1897.
3   Hambidge said he sent for the boys to do bean hoeing.
4   'A Stirring Memory of Fifty-Five Years Ago', interview with Fanny Rathband, the youngest Ascott martyr, in *The Land Worker*, December 1928.
5   http://freepages.genealogy.rootsweb.ancestry.com/~nzbound/ michaelangelo1873.htm.

ENDNOTES

6 Census for Utica, June 1, 1879–May 31, 1880
7 Pearse, Wendy (2013), 'Defiant Women — The Ascott Martyrs', *Wychwoods History: the Journal of the Wychwoods Local History Society*, Number 23, 2008.
8 Pearse, Wendy (2013).
9 Honeybone, Harry (1933).
10 Pearse, Wendy (2013).
11 See below for Eliza Honeybone's biography. She did not go to prison, but was named was on the original wooden seat around the tree on the green. She was living in Langley in 1871.
12 Honeybone, Harry (1933).
13 Honeybone, Harry (1933).
14 Honeybone, Harry (1933).
15 Higginbotham, Peter (2014). See http://www.workhouses.org.uk/life/entry.shtml.
16 McQuay, Tom and Waugh, Duncan (1996). All the information in this section about typhoid, typhus and the Pratley family is from this source.
17 Cyclopaedia Company Ltd (1903), Cyclopaedia of New Zealand, Volume 3: Canterbury Provincial District, Cyclopaedia Company Ltd, Christchurch, NZ.
18 John was the son of Eli and Frederick Pratley's half-brother John.
19 Oxford Times, 22 October 1881.
20 Oxford Times, 22 October 1881.
21 Warner, Doris (1999).
22 John Millin was one of the youths testifying against the women.
23 Cyclopaedia Company Ltd (1903), Cyclopaedia of New Zealand, Volume 3: Canterbury Provincial District, Cyclopaedia Company Ltd, Christchurch, NZ, p 893.
24 Pearse, Wendy (2013).
25 http://en.wikipedia.org/wiki/Pontypridd.
26 Pearse, Wendy (2013).
27 Arnold, Rollo (1981), p. 57.
28 Arnold, Rollo (1981), p. 58

BIBLIOGRAPHY

SOURCE DOCUMENTS

CENSUS
Census Returns of England and Wales, for the years 1841–1901, The National Archives, Kew, Surrey, England (located at www.ancestry.com).

CHURCH OF ENGLAND REGISTERS
Oxfordshire Parish Registers (transcribed onto microfiche 1994 for Oxfordshire Family History Society), containing records of baptisms, marriages and burials from the following parishes: Ascott-under-Wychwood, Asthall, Bampton, Burford, Chipping Norton, Churchill, Eynsham, Hailey, Heythrop, Kingham, Leafield, Milton-under-Wychwood, Mixbury, Over Worton, Ramsden, Shilton, Shipton-under-Wychwood, Stanton Harcourt, Swerford.

COURT DOCUMENTS
Warrant of commitment for nine of the women, 21 May 1873, CPZ 16/1, Oxfordshire Archives, Oxford County Records Office, Oxford. (This is the first charge sheet.)
Warrant of commitment for seven of the women, 21 May 1873, CPZ 16/2, Oxfordshire Archives, Oxford County Records Office, Oxford. (This is the second charge sheet.)

NEWSPAPERS
Banbury Guardian, 29 May 1873.
Jackson's Oxford Journal, May–August 1873.
Oxford Chronicle and Berks & Bucks Gazette, May 1873.
Oxfordshire Weekly News, May–July 1873.
The Times (London), January–July 1873.
Daily News, 27 May 1873; undated clippings (CPZ 16/3, CPZ 16/4, CPZ 16/35), Oxfordshire Archives.
Witney Gazette, October 1872.

BIBLIOGRAPHY

The Land Worker, December 1928.
Oxford Mail, 24 June 1977.
Evening Post, Wellington, NZ, 24 March 2001.

DOCUMENTS HELD in the OXFORD COUNTY RECORDS OFFICE
Telegram from the Secretary of State to the Governor of the County Prison Oxford, May 29 1873, CPZ 16/6, Oxfordshire Archives.
Mackenzie, William, Letter to the editor containing statements by Mary and Elizabeth Pratley regarding their treatment in prison, *The Times,* 3 June 1873,CPZ 16/8, Oxfordshire Archives.
Letter from Lord Selborne, the Lord Chancellor, to the Duke of Marlborough, the Lord Lieutenant, 4 June 1873, CPZ 16/9, Oxfordshire Archives.
Letter from A. J. Liddell to the Visiting Justices, 4 June 1873, CPZ 16/10, Oxfordshire Archives.
Letter including notice of meeting to the Visiting Justices, 5 June 1873, CPZ 16/11 and 5 June 1873, CPZ 16/12, Oxfordshire Archives.
Report of the Visiting Justices, 7 June 1873, CPZ 16/13, Oxfordshire Archives.
Reverend William Carter to the Duke of Marlborough, 14 June 1873, letter held in Oxfordshire Archives and copied from Ralph Mann's notes.
The Lord Lieutenant, the Duke of Marlborough, to the Lord Chancellor, 18 June 1873, letter held in Oxfordshire Archives and copied from Ralph Mann's notes.
Letter from Lord Selborne, Lord Chancellor, to the Duke of Marlborough, Lord Lieutenant of Oxfordshire, 26 June 1873, CPZ 16/28, Oxfordshire Archives.
Letter from Clifford Kettley on behalf of the Duke of Marlborough to J. M. Davenport, 27 June 1873, CPZ 16/29, Oxfordshire Archives .
Letter from William Mackenzie to *The Times,* 3 July 1873, CPZ 16/34, Oxfordshire Archives.

OTHER DOCUMENTS
Ascott-under-Wychwood Church of England Primary School Log Book, 1863–1887, S/09/1/A1/1, Centre for Oxfordshire Studies, Oxford.
Palmer, Edwin, 'Appeal by the Archdeacon of Oxford for the Funds to Extend the Laundry 1888', Pamphlet OXFO 365, Oxfordshire County Libraries.
Finn, Elizabeth (1987), 'The Ascott Women', unpublished essay lodged in the Oxfordshire Archives .
Ralph Mann, interviewed by Robin Thompson, reporter,*Witney Gazette,* 7 October 1982.

PUBLICATIONS

Arnold, Rollo (1981), *The Farthest Promised Land: English Villagers, New Zealand Immigrants of the 1870s*, Victoria University Press with Price Milburn, Wellington, NZ.

Baker, S. G. (1861), 'The Ascott Women', *Top. Oxon.* No 6, Spring (Item CPZ 16/37, Oxfordshire Archives, Oxford County Records Office).

Blum, Jerome (1994), *In the Beginning: The Advent of the Modern Age: Europe in the 1840s*, Macmillan, New York

Chance, Eleanor (1997), *OXFORDSHIRE of one hundred years ago*, Alan Sutton Publishing, UK.

Cyclopaedia Company Ltd (1903), *Cyclopaedia of New Zealand, Volume 3: Canterbury Provincial District*, Cyclopaedia Company Ltd, Christchurch, NZ.

Golby, J. M. (ed.) (1986), *Culture & Society in Britain 1850–1890*, Oxford University Press, Oxford.

Green, Frederick Ernest (1920), *A History of the English Agricultural Labourer, 1870-1920*, P.S. King & Son, London.

Groves, Reginald (1949), *Sharpen the Sickle!: The History of the Farm Workers' Union*, reprinted 2011 by Porcupine Press, Michigan.

Hardy, Thomas (1883), 'The Dorsetshire Labourer', reprinted in Golby, J. M. (ed.) (1986), *Culture and Society in Britain, 1850-1890: A Source Book of Contemporary Writings*, Oxford University Press, Oxford.

Hodgkins, J. R. (1978), *Over the Hills to Glory: Radicalism in Banburyshire 1832–1945*, Clifton Press, Southend.

Honeybone, Harry (1933), 'Part of the Life History of Harry Honeybone', Unpublished manuscript, held by B. McCombs, Wellington, New Zealand.

Horn, Pamela (1971), *Joseph Arch 1826–1919, the Farm Workers' Leader*, The Roundwood Press, Kineton.

Horn, Pamela (ed.) (1974), *Agricultural Trade Unionism in Oxfordshire 1872–81*, Oxfordshire Record Society, Vol. XLVIII, Oxford.

Horn, Pamela (1976), *Labouring Life in the Victorian Countryside*, Gill and Macmillan Ltd., Dublin.

Horn, Pamela (c.1998), 'Gloving by hand — a dying craft', *Limited Edition Magazine (Herts & Bucks)*, Buckinghamshire.

Jessup, Mary (1975), *A History of Oxfordshire*, Phillimore & Co. Ltd., London.

Jourdan, Sue and Richards, Sue, (1985), *The Wychwoods Album*, Wychwoods Local History Society, Shipton-under-Wychwood.

Kibble, John (1999), *Charming Charlbury with its Nine Hamlets & Chipping Norton*, The Wychwood Press, Charlbury.

Kitteringham, Jennie, (1975), 'Part 3: Country work girls in ninteenth-century England' p. 128, in Samuel, R. (ed.) (1975), History Workshop Series, *Village Life and Labour*, Routledge & Kegan Paul, London and Boston.

BIBLIOGRAPHY

Lane, Peter, and Lane, Christopher (1998), *Study Guide GCSE: History 1750 to the Present Day*, Letts Educational, London.

Leyland, N. L., and Troughton, J. E. (1974), 'Glovemaking in West Oxfordshire: the Craft and its History', *Oxford City and County Museum Publication* No.4.

McQuay, Tom and Waugh, Duncan (1996), 'A Determined Emigrant', in *Wychwoods History, the Journal of the Wychwoods Local History Society*, Number Eleven, 1996.

Mann, Ralph (c.1985), The Ascott Martyrs, unpublished notes.

Meads, Eileen (1949), *History of Chipping Norton*, Poundstone Press England.

Miller, Celia (1983), *Rain and Ruin: The Diary of an Oxfordshire Farmer, John Simpson Calvertt 1875-1900*, Alan Sutton Publishing Ltd., Gloucester.

Mingay, G. E. (1990), *Rural Life in Victorian England*, Alan Sutton Publishing Ltd., Gloucester.

Montgomery-Massingberd, Hugh (2004), *Blenheim and the Churchills*, Jarrold Publishing, UK.

Moss, Eric (1999), *Walk Humble, My Son: Growing up in Ascott-under-Wychwood 1918–1939*, Wychwood Press, Charlbury.

O'Leary, John Gerard (ed.) (1966), *The Autobiography of Joseph Arch*, MacGibbon & Kee London.

Ottewell, Gordon (2004), *The Evenlode: An Exploration of a Cotswold River*, Green Branch Press, Gloucester.

Oxfordshire Federation of Women's Institutes (1999), *The Oxfordshire Village Book*, Countryside Books, Newbury, Berkshire.

Pearse, Wendy (2013), 'Defiant Women: The Ascott Martyrs', *Wychwoods History: the Journal of the Wychwoods Local History Society*, Number 23, 2008.

Sandys, Elspeth (1996), *Riding to Jerusalem*, Hodder Moa Beckett, Auckland, NZ.

Scarth, Bob (1998), *"We'll all be union men": the story of Joseph Arch and his union*, Industrial Pioneer Publications, Coventry.

Timms, J. H. (2002) 'A Story Reminiscent of my First Plum Pudding', in *The Clipper Ship Crusader 1865–1910: Memories and Records of Over Fifty Years' Pioneering*, Cadsonbury Publications, Christchurch, NZ.

Van der Kiste, John (1986), *Queen Victoria's Children*, Alan Sutton Publishing Ltd, Gloucester.

Warner, Doris (1953), *Over the Hills to Glory*, A play registered at Stationers' Hall, London.

Warner, Doris (1999), *My Personal Memories*, Wychwood Press, Charlbury.

Webb, Mary; Spicer, Alan; and Smith, Allister (1990), *Oxfordshire Country Walks: Evenlode and Wychwood*, Oxfordshire Books, for the Oxfordshire County Council, Wheaton Publishers, Devon.

INDEX of NAMES

A

Abraham, Robert, 64, 91
Acres, Caroline, 116
Adams, Mr, 117
Alcock, William, 37
Allen, William, 46
Arch, Joseph, vii, 23, 25, 26, 27, 28, 29, 57, 58, 60, 61, 77, 78, 79, 81, 82, 86, 124, 125, 129, 136, 137
Arnold, Rollo, 132, 133, 136
Attenborough, Frederick, 29, 57, 77, 78, 125
Attenborough, Frederick Jr, 57
Attenborough, Gladys, 57
Attenborough, Harold, 57
Attenborough, John, 57
Attenborough, Mary, 57

B

Baker, R. L., 24
Baker, S. G., 136
Banbury, Gabriel, 57, 60, 61, 68, 69, 78, 79, 129
Barry, William, 44
Barter, Charles, 63
Barter, Ellen, 76
Baylis (nee Taylor), Ann, 103
Baylis, John Jr, 103
Baylis, John Sr, 103
Baylis, Joseph, 103
Baylis, Josiah, 103
Baylis, William, 103
Bayliss, Mary Ann, 94, 99
Beauchamp, Emma, 110
Beauchamp, George, 116
Beauchamp, Rachel, 116
Beauchamp, Robert, 115, 116
Belcher, (Smith), Sarah, 118
Belcher, Alan, 118
Belcher, Charles, 118
Belcher, Edward, 44
Belcher, Elizabeth, 118
Belcher, Joseph, 118
Belcher, Mary Ann, 118
Belcher, Phillis, 118
Belcher, Sarah, 118
Betteridge, Elizabeth, 159, 160
Bliss, William, 44, 46
Blum, Jerome, 136
Bowen, Superintendent, 44, 48
Bowring, Edgar Alfred, 73
Bradford, Ernest, 104
Brassey, 44
Brooks, William, 24
Bruce, Mr (Home Secretary), 66, 59, 73, 74
Butler, James, 103

C

Calvertt, John, 64
Carter, Agatha, 63
Carter, Agnes, 63
Carter, Augusta, 63

INDEX of NAMES

Carter, Edith, 63
Carter, Ellen, 63
Carter, Gertrude, 63
Carter, W. E. D., 23, 24, 37, 41, 57, 62, 63, 65, 66, 68, 70, 71, 135
Carter, William Collingwood, 63
Chaundy, John, 8, 111, 115
Churchill, Lady, 59
Churchill, Lord, 23
Clifford, F., 68
Coggins, Ellen, 11
Collins, Eleanor, 119
Coombes, Ann, 115
Cooper, Alice, 91
Cooper, James, 91
Cooper, Nathan, 91
Cooper, Nathan (b1882), 91
Cope, Superintendent, 56
Cox, Charles, 28

D

Davenport, J. M., 135
Dearing, Ann, 79
Dearing, William, 79
Dring, Alice Eva, 19, 53, 90, 91
Dring, Ann Maria, 53, 90, 91
Dring, Emma Sophia, 53, 90, 91
Dring, Hannah, 90
Dring, James, 53, 90, 91
Dring, Levia (Lavinia), 2, 5, 6, 19, 35, 37, 42, 50, 53, 55, 75, 87, 89, 90, 91, 93, 94, 96, 97, 98, 102, 103, 106, 108, 111
Dring, Mary Jane, 53, 90, 91
Dring, Samuel, 90

E

Earl Ducie, 8, 64
Edgeworth, David, 99
Edginton, Ann, 105

Edginton, Caleb, 105
Edginton, Eli, 105
Edginton, James, 105
Edginton, John, 105
Edginton, Jonathan, 105
Edginton, Jonathan (b.1827), 138
Edginton, Stephen, 105
Emmett, Ethel, 117
Esson, Mr, 194
Evans, George, 102
Evans, Harriet, 11

F

Farmer, Leah, 114
Farwell, J., 44
Finn, Elizabeth, 86, 132
Forbes, Archibald, 8, 9, 30, 58, 67, 68, 75, 76

G

Garne, George, 64
Garrard, Frederick, 115
Giles, Richard, 37
Gladstone, William, 70, 80, 81, 131
Goatley, James, 95
Goatley, Sarah, 95
Godden, Josiah, 55, 56
Golby, J. M., 124
Green, Frederick Ernest, 136
Groves, Alfred, 115
Groves, Mary, 115
Groves, Muriel, 19
Groves, Reginald, 86, 132, 136

H

Hadland, Rosetta, 109
Hambidge, George, 19
Hambidge, Robert, 20, 26, 30, 31, 32, 33, 35, 37, 38, 39, 41, 44, 45, 53, 57, 63, 65, 70, 78, 87, 93

Hambidge, Rose, 20, 32
Hancock, Charlotte, 94, 99
Hanks, Mary, 111
Hardy, Thomas, 124
Harris, Thomas, 23, 24, 37, 57, 62, 63, 65, 66, 68, 70, 71, 96
Harris, William, 102
Hart, Alfred, 114
Hart, Eliza, 114
Hart, Fanny, 114
Hart, George, 114
Hart, James, 114
Hart, John George, 114
Hart, Sarah Ellen, 114
Hart, Susannah, 114
Hayhurst, Mr, 113
Herbert, Auberon MP, 67
Hewer, William, 46
Higginbotham, Peter, 104
Hilton, Charles, 117
Hinton, Charles (b. 1898), 117
Hilton, William, 117
Hodgkins, J. R., 86, 122, 136
Hodgkins, John, 32, 33, 35, 37, 38, 39, 41, 111, 126
Hodgkins, Joseph, 46
Holloway, Christopher, 14, 37, 47, 55, 56, 59, 60, 61, 68, 77, 78
Holloway, Esther, 121
Holyfield, Thomas, 8
Honey, Jonathan, 9
Honeybone (née Cross), Millicent, 84
Honeybone (née Moss), Eleanor, 120
Honeybone (née Newman), Jane, 12, 45, 92, 100
Honeybone (née Tymms), Caroline, 120
Honeybone, Ann, 101
Honeybone, Celia, 2, 5, 120
Honeybone, Eliza, 2, 101, 120, 133

Honeybone, Elizabeth, 2, 5, 120
Honeybone, Ellen, 101
Honeybone, Emma, 101
Honeybone, Fanny (b.1855), 87
Honeybone, Fanny (b.1858), 2, 5, 7, 11, 35, 45, 50, 52, 59, 84, 86, 92, 93, 100, 114, 118, 120
Honeybone, George, 101, 102
Honeybone, George Moss, 101, 102
Honeybone, Harry, 11, 12, 20, 26, 100, 101, 123
Honeybone, Jane (b.1866), 87, 102, 120
Honeybone, John, 52, 92, 100, 101, 120
Honeybone, John (b.1869), 120
Honeybone, Kate, 87
Honeybone, Martha, 101
Honeybone, Mary, 120
Honeybone, Peter, 53, 84, 101
Honeybone, Reuban, 101
Honeybone, Sarah, 120
Honeybone, Thomas, 101
Honeybone, Thomas (b1865), 120
Honeybone, William, 114
Honeybone, William (b1814), 115, 120
Honeybone, William (b1818), 120
Honnibone, Maria, 114
Hooper, Albert, 119
Hooper, Jeremiah, 119
Hooper, Mary, 119
Hooper, Walter, 119
Hopkins, Henry, 8
Horn, Pamela, 86, 123, 124, 125, 132, 136
Hudson, George, 95
Hudson, Henry, 95
Hudson, Priscilla, 95
Hudson, Sarah, 95
Hudson, Thomas, 95
Hyatt, Richard, 8

INDEX of NAMES

J

Jackson, Thomas, 11
Jessup, Mary, 136
Jones, Dorothy, 62
Jones, Inspector, 56
Jones, Joanna Dorothea, 62
Jones, John Whitmore, 62
Jones, Lloyd, 1
Jones, Walter, 62
Jourdan, Sue, 122

K

Kench, Alice, 99, 100
Kench, Ann, 100
Kench, Annie, 100
Kerwood, Mary, 100
Kerwood, Thomas, 98
Kettley, Clifford, 98
Kibble, John, 85, 131
Kitteringham, Jennie, 14, 22, 123, 124, 136

L

Lakin, Emma, 37
Lakin, Joseph, 35, 43, 44, 48, 56, 72
Lakin, Mary, 35
Lakin, Sarah Ann, 37
Lane, Christopher, 137
Lane, Peter, 137
Langston, James Haughton, 64
Langston, Julia, 64
Lansbury, Charles, 99
Larch, Harriet, 11
Lardner (née Busby), Hannah, 89
Lardner, William, 8, 24, 53, 89, 110, 115
Lee, Mary, 9, 79
Lee, William, 9
Leggett, Joseph, 27, 55, 59, 78, 79
Lewis, Margaret, 117

Leyland, N. L., 123, 137
Liddell, A. J., 135
Long, Eleanor, 124, 135
Long, Philip, 97, 103
Longshaw, Francis, 110
Luckie, Mackenzie, 94

M

Mackenzie, William, 72, 73, 75, 135
Mann, Ralph, 58, 80, 87, 88, 122, 125, 129, 130, 131, 135, 137
Markham, George, 63
Marlborough, Duke of, 9, 50, 60, 64, 69, 70, 128, 130, 135
McQuay, Tom, 131, 133, 137
Meades, Eileen, 86, 132
Medlicott, John, 91
Metters, Mr, 117
Mildenhall, Ernest William, 91
Mildenhall, William, 91
Miller, Celia, 124, 130, 137
Millin, Emma, 113
Millin, John, 32, 33, 35, 37, 38, 39, 111, 113, 133
Mingay, G. E., 123, 124, 137
Montgomery-Massingberd, Hugh, 122, 137
Moreton, Julia, 64
Moreton, Lord, 64
Moreton, Thomas Reynolds, 64
Morgan, Gwen, 12
Morris, Frank, 103
Morris, Hannah, 9
Morris, John, 9
Morris, Joseph, 9
Morris, Mary, 103
Morris, Mary (b.1881), 103
Morris, Robert, 103
Moss (née Andrews), Hannah, 90

Moss (née Baylis), Martha, 5, 19, 35, 37, 38, 42, 50, 52, 55, 75, 93, 95, 97, 98, 99, 102, 103, 104
Moss (née Bayliss), Ann (Mary Ann), 99
Moss (née Edginton), Mary, 2, 5, 19, 35, 37, 38, 42, 50, 55, 75, 76, 87, 95, 97, 98, 100, 103, 105, 106, 116
Moss (née Honeybone) Jane, 5, 7, 11, 19, 35, 37, 38, 42, 45, 50, 52, 55, 84, 87, 92, 94, 95, 98, 100, 101, 102, 103, 105, 114, 116, 118, 120
Moss (née Hudson), Ann, 5, 35, 37, 42, 50, 52, 59, 62, 84, 87, 94, 95, 96, 98, 100, 103, 105, 116
Moss (née Panting), Emma, 98, 112, 113
Moss (née Pratley), Jane (b1790), 12
Moss (née Smith), Eliza, 16, 52, 102, 116
Moss (née Tymms), Jane, 95
Moss (née Wiggins), Ann, 102, 116
Moss (Smith), Emily, 16, 52
Moss (Smith), Mary, 5, 35, 42, 50, 87, 94, 95, 98, 100, 102, 103, 104, 105, 114, 115, 116, 118
Moss, (née Jackson), Mary, 99
Moss, Albert (b.1863), 90
Moss, Albert (b.1888), 100
Moss, Alfred (b.1834), 94, 99
Moss, Alfred (b.1836), 75, 105
Moss, Alfred (b.1896), 100
Moss, Amelia, 5, 7, 19, 35, 37, 42, 45, 50, 52, 55, 84, 87, 89, 90, 93, 94, 95, 96, 97, 98, 99, 100, 102, 103, 105, 106, 109, 111, 116
Moss, Ann Susan, 5, 35, 37, 38, 42, 50, 52, 59, 62, 89, 90, 94, 96, 97, 98, 106, 109, 111
Moss, Anna, 2
Moss, Annie (b.1893), 100
Moss, Benjamin, 99
Moss, Caleb, 52, 84, 95, 96

Moss, Caroline, 2, 5, 6, 19, 35, 37, 38, 42, 50, 52, 55, 75, 87, 93, 95, 97, 98, 100, 103, 105, 116
Moss, Charles, 98
Moss, Charles (b.1867), 90
Moss, Charlotte, 2, 5, 6, 7, 35, 37, 42, 50, 52, 59, 87, 89, 93, 94, 95, 96, 97, 98, 99, 100, 102, 103, 105, 106, 109, 111, 116
Moss, Clara, 99
Moss, Clara Esther, 112, 113
Moss, Eleanor, 120
Moss, Ellen (b.1849), 105
Moss, Emily, 16, 52
Moss, Emma (b.1835), 90
Moss, Emma (b.1870), 90
Moss, Eric, 87
Moss, Frederick (b.1885), 100
Moss, George (b.1750-8), 7, 12, 89, 94, 99
Moss, George (b.1808), 95
Moss, George (b.1826), 94, 99
Moss, George (b.1830), 45, 90, 94
Moss, George (b.1834), 112
Moss, George (b.1859), 103
Moss, George Ernest, 112, 113
Moss, Hannah, 89, 90
Moss, Harriett, 19, 52, 98
Moss, James (b.1806), 94, 98
Moss, James Charles (b.1848), 94
Moss, Jane (b.1870), 16
Moss, Jane Elizabeth (b.1825), 89
Moss, Jason (b.1838), 94
Moss, Jason (b.1840), 95
Moss, Jason (b.1843), 94, 99
Moss, Jesse (Frederick Jesse), 94, 99
Moss, John (b.1839), 90, 97, 103
Moss, Joseph (b.1804), 98
Moss, Joseph (b.1833), 90
Moss, Joshua, 52, 98
Moss, Julia, 52, 84, 90, 94, 95

INDEX of NAMES

Moss, Louisa Ellen, 105
Moss, Mary Ann (b.1868), 113
Moss, Philip (b.1826), 89
Moss, Reuben (b.1887), 100
Moss, Richard, 11
Moss, Robert, 52, 102, 103
Moss, Samuel (b.1869), 90
Moss, Thirza, 94, 99
Moss, Thomas (b.1798), 102, 116
Moss, Thomas (b.1824), 102, 116
Moss, Thomas (b.1863), 102
Moss, Walter, 87
Moss, William (b.1772), 7, 90, 94, 95, 98, 99, 102, 116
Moss, William (b.1790), 12, 89, 90
Moss, William (b.1822), 46
Moss, William (b.1824), 52, 99
Moss, William (b.1828), 12, 52, 94, 97, 99, 103, 104
Moss, William (b.1861), 90
Moss, William (b.1863), 99, 100
Mundella, MP, 66

N

Norgrove, Thomas, 44
Nunney, James, 46

O

O'Leary, John Gerard, 124, 137
Osman (née Faulkner), Maria, 53, 106, 107
Osman, (Ann) Elizabeth, 24
Osman, Ellen, 106
Osman, Emily, 106
Osman, Fanny, 106
Osman, George, 106
Osman, Maria, 53, 106
Osman, Marianne, 106
Osman, William, 106, 107
Ottewell, Gordon, 122, 137

Owen, Captain, 56
Owen, Charlotte, 97
Owen, Edward, 96
Owen, Frederick, 97
Owen, John, 97
Owen, Rebecca, 97
Owen, Susannah, 90, 96
Owen, Thomas, 97

P

Palmer, Edwin, 128, 135
Panting (née Hanks), Mary, 111
Panting, Elizabeth, 112
Panting, Emma, 111, 112
Panting, James, 112
Panting, John (b.1808), 111, 112, 113
Panting, John (b.1841), 112, 113
Panting, Richard, 112
Panting, Richard (b.1846), 112
Panting, Thomas, 111, 112
Parsons, Charles, 119
Parsons, Ethel, 119
Parsons, Frederick, 119
Parsons, Susannah, 119
Parsons, Winifred, 119
Pearse, Wendy, 133, 137
Perkins, William, 11
Phillips, Eliza, 98
Phillips, Jock, v11, 87, 122, 132
Phillips, Thomas, 98
Porter, Mr, 59
Pratley (Leafield), Jane, 2, 5, 35, 38, 105, 120, 121
Pratley (née Lidiard), Elizabeth, 43
Pratley (née Malins), Jane, 1, 83, 107
Pratley (née Moss), Jane, 23, 121
Pratley (née Moss), Jemima, 2, 8, 11, 12, 83, 90, 91, 106, 107, 112

Pratley (née Osman), Elizabeth, 5, 8, 12, 14, 35, 37, 38, 42, 43, 48, 50, 53, 55, 73, 74, 75, 76, 77, 82, 86, 96, 97, 106, 111, 135
Pratley (née Panting), Mary, 2, 5, 8, 12, 16, 35, 37, 38, 42, 43, 49, 50, 53, 55, 72, 73, 74, 75, 79, 83, 89, 97, 106, 107, 108, 111, 115
Pratley (née Shayler), Ellen, 5, 19, 35, 37, 42, 50, 52, 55, 87, 89, 96, 97, 106, 108, 111
Pratley, William (b.1796), 8, 12, 23, 106
Pratley, Albert (b.1885), 110, 111
Pratley, Alfred (b.1886), 116, 117
Pratley, Ann, 98
Pratley, Arthur Henry, 113
Pratley, Caroline (b.1872), 109
Pratley, Charles (b.1877), 116, 117
Pratley, Charles (b.1858), 12, 91, 112
Pratley, Charles (b.1875), 109, 110, 111
Pratley, Charles (b1877), 156, 157, 158
Pratley, Charles (b.1880), 104
Pratley, Charles Ernest (b.1868), 16, 53, 112
Pratley, Charles Henry (b.1897), 117
Pratley, Edward (b.1820), 116
Pratley, Edward (b.1890), 116
Pratley, Eli (b.1846), 1, 2, 4, 8, 12, 14, 23, 24, 35, 44, 53, 82, 83, 85, 91, 96, 106, 107, 108, 112, 113, 116, 126, 133
Pratley, Eli (b.1872), 14, 35, 49, 53, 55, 82, 83, 106, 107, 124
Pratley, Elizabeth (b.1869), 14, 24, 53, 82, 106, 107, 124
Pratley, Ellen (b.1871), 1, 4, 14, 53, 82, 83, 106, 107, 108
Pratley, Ellen (b.1882), 110, 111
Pratley, Emma, 23
Pratley, Ernest (b.1888), 110
Pratley, Fanny, 116, 117

Pratley, Fanny (b.1880), 121
Pratley, Frank (b.1879), 12, 14, 53, 83, 85, 91, 96, 112, 113, 114, 116, 126, 133
Pratley, Frederick James, 16, 35, 53, 85, 112
Pratley, George (b.1855), 115, 116, 117
Pratley, George (b.1874), 109, 110, 111
Pratley, George Frederick, 53, 85, 112
Pratley, George Thomas, 116, 117
Pratley, Gwendoline, 117
Pratley, Hannah, 12
Pratley, Henry (b.1883), 104, 116, 117
Pratley, James Albert (b.1861), 12
Pratley, John (b.1823), 12, 23, 24, 91, 96, 112, 121
Pratley, John (b.1850), 52, 109, 110, 111, 126, 133
Pratley, John (b1870), 109, 110
Pratley, John William, 16, 53, 112
Pratley, Joseph, 121
Pratley, Lily (b.1886), 110
Pratley, Maria (b.1888), 116, 117
Pratley, Mary (b.1879), 116, 117
Pratley, Mary (b.1836), 12
Pratley, Mary Ann (b.1870), 16, 53, 112, 113
Pratley, Mary Ann (b.1877), 113
Pratley, Philip (b.1847), 103, 105
Pratley, Philip (b.1852), 12, 112, 121, 126
Pratley, Philip (b.1877), 109
Pratley, Reginald, 117
Pratley, Rosa, 117
Pratley, Rose (b.1891), 110
Pratley, Sarah (b.1870), 103, 105, 121
Pratley, Sarah Lucy (b.1849), 12, 112, 113
Pratley, Thomas (b.1873), 16, 35, 49, 53, 55, 74, 112
Pratley, Walter (b.1885), 116, 117
Pratley, William (b.1796), 8, 12, 23, 106, 112, 123

INDEX of NAMES

Pratley, William (b.1839), 12, 23, 24, 43, 44, 45, 112
Pratley, William (b.1877), 4
Pratley, William (b.1900), 117

R

Rainbow, Thomas, 45, 102
Rathband, Ada, 92
Rathband, Alice, 92
Rathband, Edwin, 92, 93
Rathband, Frank, 92
Rathband, George, 92
Rathband, Harry, 93
Rathband, Herbert, 93
Rathband, Ida, 93
Rathband, Jane, 92
Rathband, Lily Mabel, 92
Rathband, Lizzie, 92
Rathband, Millicent, 92
Rathband, Ruben, 92
Rathband, Wilfred John, 92
Rawlinson, A. L., 37, 41, 44
Rhyman, Emma, 117
Richards, Sue, 123, 136
Robertson, Mary Ann, 95
Robinson, Eli, 29

S

Samuel, Raphael, 123
Sandys, Elspeth, 88, 132, 137
Savidge, Matthew, 64
Scarsebrook, Susannah, 7, 90, 94, 95, 98, 99, 102, 116
Scarth, Bob, 124, 137
Selborne, Lord Chancellor, 69, 70, 130, 135
Shayler (née Hadland), Rosetta, 109
Shayler, Caroline, 109
Shayler, Charles, 109
Shayler, David, 109
Shayler, Eleanor, 109
Shayler, George, 109, 110
Shayler, Hannah, 109
Shayler, Jane, 109
Shayler, Jesse, 109
Shayler, Luke, 109
Shayler, Mark, 109
Shayler, Mary-Ann, 109
Shayler, Philip, 109
Simmons, Elizabeth, 114
Simmons, Emma, 114
Simmons, Joseph, 114
Simms, George, 46
Sirman (née Honeybone), Eliza, 2, 5, 101, 120, 133
Sirman, John, 101, 120
Smith (née Belcher), Rebecca, 5, 35, 37, 38, 42, 50, 52, 53, 59, 63, 87, 92, 97, 100, 114, 118, 119
Smith (née Hart), Martha, 2, 5, 11, 35, 37, 38, 39, 42, 50, 53, 59, 92, 100, 110, 114, 115, 116, 118, 126
Smith (née Newman), Mary, 114
Smith, Allister, 137
Smith, Ann, 102
Smith, Charles, 118, 119
Smith, Charles (b.1886), 119
Smith, Eliza Emma, 63, 154, 155
Smith, Elizabeth (b.1879), 119
Smith, Elizabeth Leah, 53
Smith, Ellen Jane, 53
Smith, Fred (b.1888), 119
Smith, George, 114, 115
Smith, George (b.1868), 119
Smith, Jane Maria, 53
Smith, John, 53
Smith, Louisa, 53
Smith, Louisa (b.1876), 119
Smith, Peter, 114
Smith, Phillis (b.1874), 119

Smith, Police Constable, 24
Smith, Rachel, 53
Smith, Susannah Louise, 104
Smith, Thomas (b.1870), 160
Smith, William (b.1815), 104
Spicer, Alan, 137
Stewart, James, 95
Stewart, William, 95
Stroud, Charles, 95
Surmer, Sarah, 19

T

Taylor, Henry, 29, 55, 59, 60, 61
Taylor, Mary, 96
Thornett, Elizabeth (Betty), 7, 12, 89, 94, 99
Timms (née Newman), Caroline, 84
Timms, Ann, 84
Timms, George, 84
Timms, J. H., 125, 128, 131, 137
Timms, John, 84, 125
Timms, John Henry, 53, 84, 85
Timms, Mary, 84
Timms, Reuben, 84
Timms, William, 84
Townsend, Anthony, 8
Townsend, Thomas, 46
Troughton, J. E., 123, 137
Turner, Eliza, 98
Tweed, Penelope, 11
Tweed, Robert, 11
Tweed, Sophia, 11
Tymms, Mary, 101, 118
Tymms, Thomas, 101, 118

V

Van der Kiste, John, 129, 137
Venvill, William, 8

Victoria, Queen, 8, 35, 58, 59, 67, 129, 137
Vincent, Mathew, 29
Vorley, Harry 119

W

Walker, Charlotte, 11
Walker, Emma, 102
Walker, Frank, 102
Walker, William Jr, 102
Walker, William Sr, 102
Walton, R. M., 86, 132
Warner, Doris, 4, 19, 35, 86, 87, 110, 122, 123, 124, 126, 132, 133, 137
Waugh, Duncan, 131, 133, 137
Wavell, John, 63
Weaver, Charles, 11
Weaver, Richard, 43
Webb, Mary, 137
Westbury, Esther, 95, 112
White, Eliza, 95
White, William, 9
Whitney, Miss, 117
Wiggins, Ann, 102, 116
Wilkins, H. C., 37
Wilkins, Rebecca, 114
Williams, John, 84, 96
Williams, Martha, 84, 96
Worsley, J. H., 23, 24
Wright, Emma, 39, 41, 97
Wright, James, 97

Y

Yates, Inspector, 44, 48
York, Frances, 11
York, Samuel, 11